Retire – ge

A tongue-in-cheek version of what occurred when a bunch of uke loving seniors formed a ukulele group to 'entertain' their local community.

By Kelvin Pattison

'Retire - get a Ukulele' by Kelvin Pattison

Cover design Neil Pattison and Sarah Bonner. Stokes Bay Strummers logo by Neil Pattison Photograph on back cover by Greg Long

ISBN: 9781521476604

This work is dedicated to all current, past, and future Stokes Bay Strummers but especially to Alan Hawxwell – the founder, the heart, soul, and fun behind the Stokes Bay Strummers – passed too early and sadly missed by all who had the pleasure of his company.

This is a true story about mature men and women falling in love …. with the Ukulele.

Six years ago, a handful of bored retirees conceived and gave birth to a ukulele group, this is the tongue in cheek story of that Uke group.

All the events took place in the South of England. Some names have been changed to protect the innocent and some events may or may not have been exaggerated.

There's now hundreds of community ukulele groups across the UK and I'm sure that this story will be familiar to all of them. Take away the ukuleles and this could be the story of a choir, a knitting group, an archaeology group, or any other meeting of like-minded seniors filling time, chasing dreams, and having fun.

I need to make it clear before you read this that 'the Stokes Bay Strummers' are a fantastic group of lovely people and a great ukulele group. Stokes Bay is a truly wonderful place in Gosport on the perfect Solent. A brilliant place to live and play uke (just in

4

case these absolute truths are not clear in what follows)

For more information about the Stokes Bay Strummers see www.stokesbaystrummers.co.uk or find them on Facebook.

Contents

Chapter One – Conception

Chapter two – Falling in Love

Chapter Three – Education

Chapter Four – Birth

Chapter Five – Growing old gracefully

Chapter Six – Facing the Audience

Chapter Seven – Practice makes Perfect?

Chapter Eight – Obsession

Chapter Nine – Walking with Dinosaurs

Chapter Ten – Accompaniment

Chapter Eleven – On the road!

Chapter Twelve – David Cameron and The Stokes Bay Strummers

Chapter Thirteen – Democracy in the SBS

Chapter Fourteen – Ukulele Oblivion

Chapter One – Conception

What are busy people to do when they retire?

Engineers, ex-military personnel, civil servants, health workers, woodworkers, astronauts, nuclear physicists, tight rope walkers .... busy people, community stalwarts, mums, dads, grandmas, and grandads. All uncluttered from the world of work, all with time on their hands, hollows in their sofas, remotes with worn out buttons, well-oiled toilet seat hinges and diaries spattered with doctor's appointments. But most importantly, all with time and energy to spare.

What are the options?

Carry on working to top up the pension? Join the WI, and/or whatever the male equivalent is? Take up knitting or woodturning? Spend all one's free time looking after the grandkids? Volunteer at the local soup kitchen? Take to the settee and watch box sets. Breaking Bad, Game of Thrones or Howard's Way all in one sitting?   Work non-stop to improve the golf handicap?   Travel the world first class spending the kids' inheritance?   Take up dangerous sports or caravanning?

.... or take up Ukulele?

It's amazing, considering that Britain is the world's foremost provider of popular music and musicians, just how many frustrated older people dream to be the lead guitarist of a super group, the vocal lead in a 60's inspired pop band or even the charismatic focal point of a comedy show band. Thousands of frustrated budding Bonos or Paul McCartneys whose knuckles and ears are still smarting from the pain of recorder lessons at school.

It's a sad fact, but back in the 60's, when Britain and the Beatles were taking the musical and cultural world by storm, what did the intellectuals running our education system offer?   Recorder lessons!   In the land of the birth of pop music, thousands of 7 year olds, doing little for family harmony, trying to squeeze and squeak out 'London

Bridge' or 'Frere Jacques' if you were lucky enough to live in the leafy burbs.   To add insult to injury, hard pressed parents, less than a decade after war time rationing had ended, having to buy from their hard-earned graft (in mills and coal mines most likely) an almost unplayable stick with holes in.   Take a few minutes to imagine what the country would be like now, had Ukuleles been provided for every school child instead.

The world would be more peaceful.   Would Pete Townshend have wind-milled so violently had he played a uke?   The refresh rate on a standard 1960's 14-inch TV screen failed to cope with Townshend's swirling throbbing fender (which usually ended its life smashed – best part of £1000 down the drain).   'My Generation' better contained as a gentle rocking ukulele lilt.   The Who wearing hand knitted sweaters as guests on the Val Doonican show.

There would have been no need for Grunge, Goths or Rap. Prog rock and heavy metal would have evolved into a lighter wooden style and the NHS would be now saving millions on its' hearing aid budget.

9

Jazz, swing, pop, and reggae would have survived and flourished in this ukulele utopia and it's patently obvious that Skiffle should have been ukulele driven. Washboards, tea chests and clothes lines could then have been returned to their primary purposes.

Cliff would not have happened. Hank's wah–wah would have been severely degraded by the tremolo restrictive uke. Cliff without the Shads – don't think so.

Lonnie Donegan, Dylan, Axl Rose and Status Quo would all have been uke masters. Quo's legendary boast about knowing less than four chords, would have made them Uke supremos.

Uke officialdom confirms that Ukulele should always be acoustic; but we may (just) have allowed Clapton to plug in. It would have been a shame not to have an Eric in the uke revolution. Imagine 'Layla' blasting from a gun oiled mahogany soprano with built in pick-up.

No one can say with 100 per cent confidence what the world would be like today had the humble ukulele twanged through recent popular culture.

Smiley faces everywhere - because no one can see or hear a uke without smiling.

Less global warming - possibly.

More family harmony - maybe, but not guaranteed.

Greater equality - yes, the Uke is a great leveller.

Fewer Police Community Support Officers (PCSOs)

- they wouldn't be needed – are they needed?

Al Qaida or ISIS diverted, ukes replacing guns.

World Peace.

And another thing!

What does a devoted partner buy their bored spouse for Christmas after decades of marriage and all the socks, handkerchiefs, perfume, and gloves that this brings?   A gift that may contribute to greater harmony of the world's peoples. A gift for less than forty pounds with the potential for hours of fun and pleasure – not sure for whom – but a great gift.

Yes, you guessed – a ukulele!

Chapter two – Falling in Love

I remember the exact day I fell in love with the ukulele. Jeff Lynn and many others performed 'A Concert for George' to pay tribute to my favourite Beatle the sadly departed George Harrison. George was a little bit famous as a Beatle, but he was very famous for being a great fan of the uke. Apparently, he often told fond stories of getting together with the boys at his place and getting the ukes out. I used to think about this often when enduring our music shop's lack of grandeur. Was George a better uke player than me simply because he practiced in surroundings much better attuned to creativity? Anyway, at this concert, Joe Brown, with a microscopic soprano ukulele tucked almost under his chin, played an immensely moving farewell to his friend George. This for me, and I suspect for many others, was the moment that the ukulele came alive. 'I'll see you in my dreams' sang by Joe Brown with his customary warm wide grin and unnaturally full head of spiked hair. His love for George and the obvious loss he felt, shining through in a truly moving musical event. His arrangement based on the sweetest little uke riff. Even on this tiniest of instruments this riff pierced through the electric guitars and strings massed behind Joe Brown at the Albert Hall. From that day, I wanted a ukulele. Well actually I wanted to play Joe Brown's version of *'I'll see you in my dreams'*. Ukulele players all over this country have been trying to replicate this song in that style ever since.

My wife must have noticed my moist eyes during the concert because the following Christmas she bought me my first ukulele, a Tanglewood soprano in rich mahogany – purchased in the days when the Gosport music shop was a solid business. I've learned since that the gift was a bit of a joke. My wife has suffered, nee endured much because of this joke. Talk about golfing widows is nothing compared to the time that this tiny instrument has filled in my dotage. I've also spawned two boys who have grown up to be reasonable guitar players and both with an outstanding knowledge and love of popular music. They were not impressed on two levels. Firstly, the ukulele in their view, is not a real instrument. Why haven't they seen *'A Concert for George'* I ask myself? Moreover, they envisaged many embarrassing moments ahead as Dad tried to play this stupid shrunken four stringed monstrosity in public or even worse at family

14

gatherings.   Truth is, I would have preferred hankies or socks. I would have gotten greater satisfaction from being presented with an Oxfam certificate to say that I had provided a goat for a struggling Afghan family for a year.

By Boxing Day I still couldn't play *'I'll see you in my dreams'*. I couldn't even tune the damn thing – GCEA what's that all about?   Must be wrong, it's got to go 'low to high' surely – 're-entrant tuning' sounds like a training course for immigrants.

My dog didn't have fleas at this stage.

Fortunately, this frustration was short lived, and by Easter the front room was filled with something that sounded a bit like that good ole cowboy lament 'Streets of Laredo'. The following summer my shed, once full of tools and fragrant off-cuts of wood collected over a life-time of hording, became crammed with uke song books and DVDs. I searched in vain for the much-needed Kamikaze Uke Method book. 'Jumping Jim', 'Ukulele Ike' and his relative 'Ukulele Mike', 'Roy Smeck's Magic Uke Book', 'Guckert's',

'The Peter Pan Method book', 'Cliff Edwards' and 'Bert Weedon's play in a day' (when I almost threw the uke out of the window to go back to trying guitar) 'Hum & Strum' … nothing was helping, arghh!

On reflection, I would summarise that song books and YouTube are generally good - DVDs are generally bad.   You can tell by the dodgy dress sense and the inane grins on the faces of the people on the covers of these so-called self-learn DVDs that the presenters don't have much of a social life or talent for teaching.   A one hour DVD, half of that covering the tuning, a middle section on London Bridge and then straight into six fingered rag time triple strumming – just because they can, it's a power thing.

On your own, in the confines of one's mortgage free baby boomer abode or shed, strumming your ukulele can seem somewhat sordid.   The immortal words 'I'm off to my shed to strum my ukulele' always raises eyebrows and nods and winks.   Better on your own I say, rather than persecuting your whole family. The big issue is that a learner playing uke with no vocal accompaniment sounds bloody awful. Not as bad as a learner uke player who is tone deaf and still singing though.   It's a fact of ukulele-ing that strumming and singing must, most the time, occur simultaneously. For the aged beginner, this is the uke equivalent of rubbing your tummy and patting your head.   Not easy when one is concentrating so intensely on the spotty YouTube youth – Ukulele Mike or Smouldering Sid Strummer or some other oink that's taken you 50 minutes to find on the dodgy wi-fi connection in your bedroom since the signal in these parts is not strong enough to reach the outdoor shed. Sitting, hiding, on the edge of the bed thrashing squeaky chords and singing 'You are my Sunshine' off key, is a ritualistic passage of honour that all uke players must pass through.

Then the eureka moment!

I can strum a few chords, but the singing is still bloody awful, so why not get some else to do the singing. Most of us by this stage will have asked our spouse, our children or even our grandchildren to provide this essential service. Thing is, they can't do it.   They can never follow that semi-rhythmic uke strumming delivered with all the coordination of a traffic jam akin to a toddler discovering a rattle in his hands for the first time. They think that they know the correct version of the song, but what they don't know is *your* version. Your version is special. It is played at a special tempo and includes integral hesitation breaks to allow chord change fingering. B minor – don't get me started on that mother! Another major issue, or advantage for some later year beginners is that one's spouse may sometimes be a little 'Mutt and Jeff' – which doesn't help you – but may provide a perfect protective lifeline for them.

Still I was falling in love. I was having an affair with my lovely little uke.

It always rains on August Bank Holiday Monday in Gosport, but thousands still turn out to traipse round soddened local fares and events. It was at one of these events that I met with an old colleague who had heard on the grapevine that I was trying to learn uke – so was he. He declared that a few like-minded delusional people were signing up for beginner's uke lessons and even worse, thinking about forming a ukulele group.

'Not for me – no way. I'm not strumming in public. I only strum my instrument in the dark, in the safe space that is my bedroom'.

'Come on what's the issue?'

'You'll need a hobby in four or five years' time, there's going to be a bloody awful financial crisis* and you'll be made redundant (I'm not bitter – honest).

'Imagine how much more palatable this will be (because it will happen) if you were part of a lovely caring local group to fill your time?'

'But I can't sing!'

'Course you can, everyone can sing'

'I can't'

'Come along to the Music Shop tonight – give it a go'

'OK then ………but I'm not singing!'

[*This could have been the first time that the financial crash was predicted, imagine how life would have been – no crash and no Gosport uke group – doesn't bare thinking about]

'There's only one answer. You are going to have to make the effort. Get off your backside, open the front door, venture out to meet likeminded people. I'm a nice guy, I'm sure all ukulele beginners will be equally nice. Go and find some, and together, you can master this instrument, it can't be hard to learn – children do it!'

Adult education classes, don't get me started on this. Confused seniors, out of their comfort zones, trying to learn or more likely, filling time slots in their sad boring pointless existences. Bricklaying or plumbing - why? There's thousands of perfectly good young fit trades people out there. Get your wallet out and give them the work. Get it done properly for Pete's sake.

Learn French or Italian? Don't bother. We Brits have mastered the art of speaking English loudly and getting everything we need in any country in the world. 'Please', 'thank you' and 'two beers', 'four' if you have friends who will still travel with you, is enough in any foreign language. Anyway, European languages have been condemned as obsolete in the post-Brexit confusion. It may well have to be Mandarin or Japanese in the future – both beyond the average retiree's brain. Maybe the plan is to develop our own language post Brexit. The world has stolen and polluted English and in this new non-caring, non-sharing age we may need a new language only understood by people who have lived in the UK for at least a generation if we are to achieve the wishes so clearly articulated in the referendum and push toward total isolation *(sorry, too much ranting politics, too soon)*.

Photography, forget it, it's all digital now. Yoga and palates likewise, you'll do yourself an injury. Now something that could just possibly lead to fulfilling your duvet dreams of becoming a musical god – that would be a truly worthwhile time filler. What could that be?

Yes, you guessed – ukulele classes!

Books have ceased to exist, replaced by Kindles, Tabs, and Pads. By the time anyone reads this, all local libraries may have been demolished to make way for unaffordable affordable housing. However, if one travels a bit further, collecting a few more notches on the bus pass *(still available at the time of writing, but don't hold your breath, Baby Boomer benefits may not survive the next surge of tabloid jealousy)* and visit the next town big enough to maintain some vestige of public service, you may find, or be discovered, by a 'Discovery Centre'.

What the hell is a Discovery Centre?

A Discovery Centre is the PC name for a library in our neighbourhood. Well, it's like a library, with books and everything. It's a library spared from swingeing cuts. It may have had a lick of paint, new signs and a carpet fitted. It has been spared by the self-interested county councillors in order to appease the last few intelligent local tax payers who still have the inclination and wit to vote at local elections. No, to be fair, it is different, the 'Discovery Centre' has a coffee franchise and contributes to the local health agenda by selling cakes. One can 'Discover' what it is like to buzz on caffeine and sugar. But more to the point the Discovery Centre now has classes, and yes you guessed

...Ukulele beginner classes!

For those that don't know - Ukuleles make a noise. Libraries (hush my mouth – Discovery

23

Centres) still bask in the splendour of 'shush'. Racks of beech shelving straining under heavy, dusty historic collections and the only smart kid in the town, cramming to get a university place. Four blue rinsed Librarians perched behind walnut counters *(austerity cuts haven't yet totally culled this rare breed because Librarians are a protected species since they have years of education and a degree in librarianship - all to stamp books and shush)*. Shush and Uke classes? Not a wholly cohesive mix.

Do you remember the time, pre-Amazon, when every small town had a music shop? Well-meaning musicians who kept the wolves at bay by selling instruments to pushy parents and bored children and by providing music lessons to stroppy bored kids. One could purchase Bert Weedon's *'Play Guitar in a Day'* book (pre-trade's description I think). You got the instrument of your choice demonstrated by some outrageously and annoyingly talented spotty youth and then you took a turn. This little cameo was taking place all over the land and we now know that it was pre-designed and rehearsed solely to embarrass the prospective purchaser into parting with cash. The six fingered 14-year-old music shop assistant would

24

thrash out an immaculate 'All around the Watch Tower' with effects and tricks that even Hendrix hadn't mastered and then hand the instrument back to the customer 'to have a go'. Well, what does one do? Can't remember the chords from 'London Bridge'? Not sure which hand to strum with? Suddenly developed the coordination of a traffic jam and the ear of Les Dawson. There's only one way out. Give the instrument one firm, slow, deliberate down strum – only one – then get yer wallet out - you've purchased. Get out of the shop quick, back on the bus, put the strange shaped box on the parcel shelf and ignore the unease of your fellow passengers. Why do musical instrument boxes always look as though they could house a sub-machine gun?

Well, our town had a Discovery Centre and a Music Shop – how's that for a fantastical accident of musicality and geography?

To be frank the owner of the music shop had the business brain of Joey Essex and lived a lifestyle akin to a vagrant. Thus, he was always broke and always in crisis. Could his lack of talent for business be compensated for by a talent for teaching ukulele? Could the latest uke surge provide sufficient retired cannon fodder to pay enough (for uke lessons) to save the music shop business? No, as we will later learn. However back in the day, eight or nine budding Claptons gathered at the back of the Discovery Centre to commence 'beginners' ukulele'. Forty quid for ten weeks' instruction, two hours a week. 'Down - up, down-up, down-up, down-up'; and 'Down-up, down-up, down-up' – sometimes played using the bluffers best weapon – the air strum. Remember these lessons were in a library – shush!

That was the start of it all. The pop strum and a waltz strum perfected - right hand sorted. Chords next. Tricky things chords. Sixty-year-old arthritic fat fingers 'dancing' across a fret board no bigger than a bread knife – and just as sharp on some of the ukes sold at the Gosport music shop. I met a 'uke player' a few years later who boasted that he never bothered with the chords. Never put his left hand on the uke – too complicated – 'all you need is the strum'.

Best chord of all on the uke is the C chord. The people's chord. One finger (any one will do, let's not complicate things) plonked snuggly on the third fret, well away from the other annoying strings, and strum that heavenly chord with ease. Thus, any song with a predominance of the people's chord gained early popularity among the beginner's class (and remained in the repertoire for many years afterwards to be honest). Ten weeks, four chords, two strumming patterns, friendships bonded and the shush library rule buried forever. I'm told that the library, sorry, The Discovery Centre, now runs courses in pneumatic drilling, double bass drumming and air raid warning siren appreciation.

'You are my sunshine' and 'Cotton fields' in the bag - rendered in a strangely satisfying morose and hesitant style – not unlike an eighties hip-hop band or Morrissey in his heyday. The group sometimes even managed to finish playing a song all at the same time. We never started at the same time, but the library was all whoops and cheers, when and if by accident, we all ended together – happy days!

27

The teacher's financial security continued to spiral downwards and letting this cash-cow go was not a pleasant thought. What next?   'Intermediate ukulele lessons'?   I don't think so. More than 50 years since some of this lot attended any form of education or training. As many ukulele wives have since confirmed, this lot were un- trainable. It would have been easier to get a bunch of geese to harmonize Danny Kaye songs. It would have been easier to train your 5-year-old grandson to build a functioning nuclear reactor. Have you ever tried to get 8 or 9 stroppy grumpy old men and women to do anything in unison – apart from moan that is! Ten weeks was stretching the grey matter a little too far – so it was back to the sofa to catch up on Corrie.   This could have been a sad loss to the musical world. Would the residents of numerous Gosport care homes never drink from this newly filled talent pool?

Entrepreneurs have ideas. 'I know' said the desperate music shop owner/teacher entrepreneur. 'I have a music tuition room in the back of my shop on Stoke Road. Why don't we meet there once a week?' Sub-text - then you could keep paying me a few quid, I could occasionally buy some food and my business

28

may just survive. Maybe out of sympathy or social awareness the 'founder members', as they later became known - much to the annoyance of newer members, agreed to meet on Thursday evenings at the music shop tuition room at the back of the shop.

Now, Stoke Road is not the most up-market area of Gosport. Gosport, although lovely, is probably not the most up-market area on the south coast. The music shop was probably not the sleekest music shop on the planet, but it did have some instruments. The music shop tuition room, as it turned out, wasn't even a room. It had electrical power sometimes, one 13-amp socket, but only if the bill had been paid. Only once did a strummer plug his uke amplifier into the mains, and it's only Specsavers entry into the hearing aid business that partially rectified the consequences of this foolhardy move. The room had lighting, but members soon learned that it was probably wisest to bring your own. A sight that will live long in our memories, elderly Strummers trying to play with only each other's head torch for illumination. One week the lights failed completely, or the bill hadn't been paid and the utility company switched off the supply. The unrealistically enthusiastic emergent Strummers didn't let this put them off. We were in a shop and shops

29

have shop windows facing the street.   Streets have street lights. So about ten determined Strummers sat in the shop window to borrow the street light and carried on learning stoically, much to the bewilderment and amusement of the passing locals.

The shop never had heating, apart from a mangy old dog. Several female members would bring in tit-bits for the dog and in return it would lay on their feet to keep them snug. This backfired one week, when unknowingly to the strummer, the dog discovered the tit-bits in her cardigan pocket and eat though the wool (or whatever Primark cardigans are made of in Gosport) to get at the food. The strummer didn't find out until she got up to go and the cardigan unravelled across the floor.   The shop owner of course volunteered to pay for the half eaten cardi, which was immediately upgraded by the quick-witted strummer from Primark to M&S.

With no heating and winter cardigans getting eaten, strumming faster was the only way of generating warmth. To this day, this is the most likely reason, as to why the group plays *'Donald where's your Troosers'* at a speed that could make a Scotsman's sporran self-combust. This venue had chairs, but one had to brave the store room to find a seat capable of supporting an adult's weight. It had some 'walls', a ceiling and lots of doors leading to who knows where. It didn't have heating, but it did have carpets - not on the floor - but on all the vertical walls. This, we were told, was for 'acoustic reasons' and not to hide the lack of paint or plaster or the damp. Maybe the carpets had been taken up from the floor to deter the carpet fleas; or maybe the carpet fleas had had enough of the cold floor and had gotten together to drag the carpets up the walls in some desperate bid for sanctuary. In fact, the carpeting, now on the wall, had been donated by a sympathetic strummer to the destitute music shop owner for use in his flat. He had of course prioritised its use for the good of music – or he'd been thrown out of this flat – we never knew.

Strummers soon began attending sessions with their trousers tucked into their socks. Those who didn't could be recognized down the High Street by the bites decorating their ankles. Some said that there was a toilet behind one of the doors and through yet another 'store room'. Personally, I don't know how true this myth is. Most of the group never dared use the toilet, or even talk about it. One strummer was deeply shocked that the shop owner's grubby grey grundies were on full view drying over the toilet radiators. A common occurrence in Gosport, so why the shock? No something else was amiss. We had one member with an unpleasant medical condition, not uncommon among the Strummers, and he had to use the toilet frequently. Even he avoided the shop loo on most occasions. One week after squeezing his bladder with the butt of his tenor uke for over an hour in a vain attempt to stop the flow, he donned his headlight torch and dashed off to find the shop toilet. He was never the same man, and even to this day blankly refuses to discuss his experience.

All this for only two pounds a session. And yes, you have guessed - price ruled the day. The Strummers would have moved practice to a urine processing factory had one been available for 50p less than the music shop. Before each session could begin, teacher would collect the two quid, recommend that the group practice some strumming patterns while he took his newly gathered dosh across the road to Waitrose to buy sustenance for himself. Hard to

32

believe, even in these days of poverty and austerity, but yes, it's true, Gosport has a Waitrose!

This process was particularly touching on the many weeks when the teacher combined his teaching with his child care responsibilities. A great tonic for the elderly Strummers to be told by a seven-year-old that they are making an awful noise.

Still despite the surroundings these were happy days. All the Strummers have very fond memories, even love for these times. Countless times I drove away from those sessions with tears of laughter and an aching stomach brought on by the experience of trying to strum and sing together. It doesn't sound difficult, does it? It's not, and its great fun. Taking part with good friends and sharing laughter is a great tonic. The music shop owner was a superb musician and an excellent teacher. There is no doubt that his early tuition set the musical foundations for all future Strummers. Many would turn the clock back and attend at the music shop again. Sadly, this is not possible. The internet finally killed the business, probably just before the owner would have done so himself.   He moved away and the shop is now a photography studio.   I don't know if the toilets have been improved or if they ever even existed!

In the autumn of 2010, in the foresaid music shop tuition room, the group was born and lifetime bonds made. We had started out on the road to making fools of ourselves in public. There was no choice. Two of the founder members, an over enthusiastic married couple, had accepted a booking for a 'gig' in a few weeks' time. We needed a name, a set list, a uniform, a logo, a constitution ...... and oh yes, we may need to be able to play the uke and sing at a level whereby we could just about get away with our self-respect intact.

This was serious. The first gig was imminent - a foolish risk? The Mayor and local council dignitaries were gathering at a local council run hotel and we were to be the after lunch 'entertainment'. Focus was the key. Members of the group had succeeded professionally at high levels of management and business in their working lives - so 'focus' and 'delivery' and 'meeting deadlines' was engrained into the emerging group. So, down to business. The business in question is obviously to practice playing

35

the uke and singing. I've lost count of the frustrating hours spent longing to strum, fingers poised over the strings. There have been practice nights when the uke could have stayed at home in its' cosy warm case. It was established very early in the groups' evolution, that 'stray strumming' whilst someone (anyone) was talking must be severely dealt with. Many members have been on the receiving end of the 'death stare' and had a razor sharp 'shush' drilled into their lug-holes before an emergent strum had hit the second string. 'Talking about playing', taking priority over 'playing', is a common ukulele phenomenon; probably because some people in the group are more skilled in the former. So, we had our first gig in a few days' time and what was the first thing discussed? A discussion which took up all the first practice session. Yes, you guessed – choosing a name for the group.

Remember these were very keen, intelligent stalwarts of the community and not the usual type to try and 'wing it'. But the fact that we could only muster three chords between us, could not strum and sing at the same time and had never tried to play together was a secondary issue.

'Ukes of Hazard' – it has to be, great name, says it all'

'I don't get it - what does it mean?'

'it's a play on a 70s USA cop show – Dukes of Hazard'

'What's that got to do with us?'

'we're a ukulele group, not a cop show'

'How about 'The Seekers?'

'Sorry taken already, 50 years ago'

'Strummers' then that's more ukulele,

And a bit less cop and a bit less 60s'

'Yes, but there's lots of Strummers around

– we need something unique'

'What about 'The Pluckers' then?'

'I'm not plucking, I'm strumming!'

'There's a group across the water in darkest Portsmouth I think they've called themselves 'The Pompey Pluckers'

'Well they can keep it then – silly name anyway'

'No, we need something that ties us to Gosport'

'I don't want to be tied to Gosport it's a shit hole,

I live in Fareham'

'I love Gosport, Fareham's a shit hole.'

'Sorry chaps going to have to hurry you, the power's due to go off in 7 minutes and I need to make up my bed in the back of the shop'

'Ok 'The Gosport Strummers' it is then'

'No – too down market'

'I've got it, how about 'The Stokes Bay Strummers' – that's got a romantic lilt to it, sound almost Californian and Stokes Bay is just over the road and we are in Stokes Road'

'And that would mean we are the SBS – sounds like a real killer organization – yes, we love it!

So, the one and only, world famous Stokes Bay Strummers were christened. We had a name. No one will ever know the story had 'The Ukes of Hazard' emerged from that first meeting. Some five years after, a member declared that since many of us live in Lee-on-the -Solent (the posh area of Gosport) he had wanted the name to be 'Kings of Lee-on' – if only he'd spoke up at that first meeting. Another later suggestion was 'Turks Town Twangers'. 'Turks Town' is an historical reference stemming from a time when Turkish prisoners of war were held in Gosport. However, this is now seen as a disparaging term manly used by people from Portsmouth (Portsmouth also known as 'Pompey'). In fact, Turks Town was probably suggested by an undercover Pompey Plucker so not acceptable on any level.

Reputations secured and name sorted, so all agreed that the next meeting must be about the music. 'Bring your ukes there's a chance we may play them soon'.

The first gig was to be a 20-minute slot and it was figured that with a bit of banter (banter – what banter?) between each, about five songs would suffice. Those early days were very straightforward. After a few years, we had hundreds of songs to choose from but in preparation for that first public performance we needed five songs, each with chords we could play and move between without too much teeth sucking or having to refocus the bifocals locked at less than 6 inches from the frets. Great if all the songs could also include the good old peoples' chord, the blissfully easy 'C'. In fact, C, G and G7, even at this early stage, were all attainable by 80 percent of the group, 80 percent of the time. Three chords an absolute luxury. Did you know that one of the greatest rock and roll songs of all time, Chuck Berry's *'You never can tell'* has only two chords and yes, we could play both? However, have you ever tried to sing that song? It may only have two chords but the lyrical and vocal work is very complex. No one had Chuck Berry on speed dial (and it's doubtful he would have travelled to Gosport, after all it was only our first gig, and it's more than likely that we hadn't yet had much publicity on Beale Street, downtown Memphis, Tennessee). Sadly, Chuck Berry has now passed away and we will never master 'You never can tell'. Joe Brown's *'I'll see you in my dreams'* was still a dream too distant. So, the first ever set list comprised of the only songs we could almost play, and looked like this….

'You are my sunshine

Cotton Fields

Bring me sunshine

Summertime

Five Foot Two, Eyes of Blue'

.... wow, standby Ticketmaster, and eBay there's going to be a ticket rush for this gig.

It's worth noting at this point, that to the best of our knowledge the creators of all these songs have long demised. This tradition of only playing songs written by people that are definitely deceased is still close to the hearts of the Strummers. This is nothing to do with copyright issues, nor is it fear of litigation by some sharp 'no win no fee' US attorney. It may just be that 'older' people choose older songs to play to other 'older' people. Trying to drive the Strummers to play modern songs, or even songs by artists still alive, is a futile and frustrating occupation – more of this later.

Our first 'gig'. This word is very much an over dramatisation at this point in our development. Noel Gallagher 'gigs', Dylan 'gigs' even the Bee Gees 'gigged' – we couldn't hope to 'gig'. Was it a lunch time concert? Well the Bournemouth Philharmonic and probably even Nigel Kennedy play lunch-time concerts. Let's call it what it is – 'Care in the Community'. Six or so retired seniors attempting to entertain. None of them at their peak and few of them in full control of all their bodily functions and faculties. These people at best needed support or at worst care in their local community. It was therefore very apt that the first gig was in a local function room supported and attended by local councillors. A very sympathetic caring audience - hopefully.

We even had a dress rehearsal – the first and only time in the group's history. Twenty minutes before strum off, we were all gathered in a tiny room to run through the songs. This was after a stiff drink at the bar, tuning our instruments seven times each (yes,

43

we even tuned our instruments – pros!) and a group hug in the toilets. To our shock and horror someone from the venue came into the room and videoed our rehearsal – talk about pressure. To this day no one knows what happened to this first recording of the Stokes Bay Strummers. One day someone may discover it and it may become as famous as that crackly first Elvis recording of 'That's all right mamma' in RCA Studio B, Nashville. Back to reality, the five songs were rehearsed and the total time played - just over four minutes. One would think that nervous tension would limit and slow the strumming arm, Not the case. Nerves, not helped by the overly intrusive video man, resulted in each song being delivered at autobahn speed. Normal running time for this eclectic collection of songs should be about 12 minutes. After years of playing we still tend to race through songs when a little nervous. But also, poor singing, and poor playing can be ameliorated by strumming and singing a bit faster – we think or hope. 'Calm down Strummers' – 'We'll be going off before we're going on' - 'take a breath' – 'take a chill pill'*. We will be OK just need to stick together, deep breaths, relax and don't stop smiling.

[*please note that drug use is not part of the Stokes Bay Strummers culture. Stokes Bay Strummers wish to make it clear that it does not tolerate or condone recreational or gig related drug use – apart from, that is, the rucksack full of prescription drugs each Strummer needs to keep their many and varied ailments at bay– such a drain on the NHS.]

The Mayor and local council dignitaries were gathered. The after lunch 'entertainment' was about to start. We had a new plan. One of our better singers would sing the verses to 'You are my Sunshine' and the remaining tuneless masses would only join in on the choruses. We had practiced, we had even rehearsed and were quietly confident that we could now all start at the same time. Our emerging leader had taken counting lessons and he could do 1,2,3, or 1,2,3,4. Only problem being that we were never sure when it should be a 3 count of a 4 count. Anyway, we all started playing at the same time and the lead singer started singing at exactly the right time – a bloody miracle. The fault line began cracking however when due to an overwhelming attack of stage fright, the lead singer started on the chorus instead of the verse. The

45

group remained in auto and carried on strumming the verse chords. On the changeover from chorus to verse or vice a versa no one knew where we were. At the end of the song, or at a place where the pain stopped for both entertainers and the entertained, we waited for the applause. Not a ripple. One would think that locally elected community champions, the mayor and council officials paid for by the community would have shown some appreciation. OK it wasn't Band-Aid but I've seen worse on BBC's Play School.

We had music sheets of course we did. We'd even been out and bought music stands. Do you remember music stands from school? Horrendous contraptions that either take the tip of your finger off when trying to unravel them or get completely seized up and in need of serious bending to open them. We proudly walked out in front of those dignitaries in that sumptuous council venue that day carrying our music stands aloft as though we were walking on to the Albert Hall stage to deliver the last night of the proms. We had tried to minimize the number of stands but this was met with great apprehension. We soon learned that the novice strummer needs his own stand as a security prop and never could we trust sharing music sheets. Those individual annotations we had all made

46

on our sheets could be the difference between an ordinary performance or a blockbuster Freddie Mercury moment. Six Strummers equals six music stands – it's the Law. The other thing you may remember about the music stands from school is how easily they fall over. Extreme nerves played a part and one stand toppled and the other followed like a row of dominoes. A great start to the concert .... for a comedy circus group.

The rest of the concert or gig or entertainment or community therapy remains lost in a blur of emotion and acute embarrassment.

Those six founder Strummers have never quite been the same since that day. The Strummers have now played more than 250 gigs, but those six brave and foolish trail blazers still break out in a cold sweat prior to each new gig as they relive their first gig memories.

Chapter Five – Growing old Gracefully

Yes, you read it right, 250 plus gigs completed. How can this be? Is it the result of some amazing marketing phenomenon? How, why, and where could a bunch of deluded seniors play all these gigs? Well unbelievably that first gig became the foundation stone in a growing reputation for the Strummers. Agents from many local venues were on the phone to our self-appointed secretary to book us. Landline, not mobile phone – too new-fangled. All Strummers maintain a 'mum and dad' landline so that their offspring know it's them ringing since only mums and dads still have a landline. When I say 'venues' I predominantly mean old peoples' homes (residential care and nursing – no discrimination in the Strummers), and sheltered accommodation sites. When I say 'agents' I mean 'carers'. In our first year, we visited more care homes than a Care Quality Commission inspector.

Note to self – if or when I'm a resident in a care home please stop feeding, watering me, and changing my pants if the weekly entertainment is a visiting ukulele group. Switch of my life support, give any remaining money I've failed to spend to avoid my children inheriting, to the local council to help better fund Social Care. Maybe the earnings from ukulele groups across the country could also go toward funding Social Care, because it won't have any Government funding the way things are going.

The best thing about entertaining in a residential home is the captive audience. They are locked in, no choice. We played in one home where the residents had been plied a strange red liquid served from gigantic demi-john jars bubbling away in the centre of the room. Don't know if this was 'wine' since we didn't get a chance to partake but it was certainly doing the residents a lot of good. One elderly man shuffled up to us after our concert to tell us that this had been the best night's entertainment of his life. Very touching and very sad in equal measures. Note to family – take me out more while you can and if you ever put me in a home make sure it's one that dishes out liberal measures of this red gloop. We accepted a weekly residency at one care home. A residency at a care home is a dangerous concept for us baby boomers. Our time is not too distant. At first, we were playing old time tunes, *'Five Foot Two', 'Moonlight Bay'* *and 'Sweet Georgia Brown'* etc. Although our average audience member may have looked old and may have had serious health and mobility issues, we soon realized that many of them had developed their musical preferences in the 1960's. The Beatles, Stones, American R&B and Soul is what they wanted, and most importantly, what got them singing and joining in. In all seriousness, I must say that we have had some exceptionally enjoyable times in many care homes and brought much joy to many people.

It's not been obvious on occasions who needs the services of the care home, the Strummers, or the residents. Looking down the line of Strummers and then out to the audience it can be difficult to distinguish. We've often had to wait, strumming arms coiled like springs whilst care staff finish the bingo or organize the raffle. During one such gig, our favourite and most elderly strummer became morose when he realized that none of his tickets had been drawn in the raffle. Hardly surprising to the rest of us, since he had kept the tickets and the stubs rather than putting the stubs in the raffle drum. We put his name down for the next available room.

Then there was the time just prior to playing 'Valerie' (yes, I know a modern(ish) song). We always ask if anyone in the home is called Valerie then we could dedicate the song to her. We also ask if anyone's called 'Glad' prior to the most famous Dave Clark Five song so we can arouse the audience with 'feeling Glad all over' innuendo. Anyway, after announcing 'Valerie' and calling for anyone called Valerie, no one came forward, so we thrashed out the song in true Zutons style (must be Zutons, never Amy Winehouse). We'd played about three more songs when a lovely old lady appeared from nowhere right in front centre stage. Awe how sweet we thought, it's taken Valerie all this time to respond, but no …. she thought she'd won the raffle and was asking us for her prize!

We soon learned that a sleeping audience is no bad thing. I once slept through a whole Tom Paxton concert. I've never had the inclination to attend a James Blunt gig, but if I ever feel insomnia coming on I would try one out. We soon learned to carry on regardless of whatever was happening in front of us. One or two residents falling asleep and sliding off their chairs onto the floor was not an uncommon occurrence, and the staff were well used to it. One carer told us that she needed to come into the room with us when we start to play. At first, we thought that this was some sort of CRB or Government safeguarding requirement, but no, it was a more fundamental issue. One of the residents apparently gets violent under certain conditions. 'What conditions?' we ask, 'oh only when she hears music'. Well you can imagine this posed quite a dilemma for us. It wasn't only the prospect of violence (although we still had big Mike and big Frank with us at this stage) it was the fear that the unfortunate resident may not recognise what we were doing as 'music'. We needed therefore a violent reaction that day. We hadn't yet begun to call ourselves musicians – although we were on the way to six chords, 20per cent of the group could now squeeze out a B flat (a tricky and very aspirational uke chord) and some of the group could sing almost in tune. We hadn't realised, but we craved recognition as musicians and it was thankfully forthcoming, when after the first song, the resident in question stormed forward toward one of our lady singers shouting, 'shut up - you old bag!'. Very sweet and much more rewarding and satisfying than any future Grammy Award or Platinum Disc.

At one of your usual venues, one elderly gentleman got up and walked out of the room as soon as we started – we were quite good by this time, so quite an insult. However, he returned a minute or two later, with a copy of the Daily Mirror in his hand, and sat back down in his chair in front of the band and proceeded to hold the paper up in front of him for the whole performance, effectively blocking out the band. When we finished, he put the paper down. He did this every time we played at this venue. Did he enjoy the show, were we providing a valuable social service or were we just getting right on his nerves? We never knew.

On another occasion, we had only played one or two songs, when, a severe looking little lady got up out of her seat where she had been listening to us, came forward and stood in front of the group and proceeded to inform us that she would be instructing her solicitor to have us thrown out of the Nursing Home, and that we were to stop playing immediately. She was so well dressed and so eloquently spoken that this speech completely threw us and we were all rather confused for some 20 seconds or so until one of the Nursing Staff interrupted her and got her sat down again. I imagine that threats of legal action where common place for The Who, Pink Floyd and The Pistols but surely not for us. We were committing some musical crimes, but nothing that would have stuck in Gosport Magistrates court I'm sure. Although we came close on one occasion. One of our new members, had a very realistic Dracula costume, complete with make-up and appropriate hair-style. A great costume for our Halloween gig at a local residential home – had he turned up at the correct address. He knocked on the door of a neighbouring private house, and announced to the horrified owner, that he, dressed as Dracula, was here to strum his uke for her.

We always throw ourselves into any event and need no excuses to get dressed up. It's amazing how sober upright pillars of the community take to cross-dressing and dressing up. These people must have whole wardrobes of dress up clothes. God knows what goes on behind their closed doors. So, for many concerts hats and wigs would come out. Most of the male Strummers are bald and it's quite a thermal challenge to continue singing and strumming in a care home with thermostats set at nuke level eleven, whilst wearing a hat and wig.

We had tartan for Scottish themed gigs including three-foot diameter tam o' shanter tartan hats and one member even appeared in a pair of his wife's tartan slacks. This turned out to be a big mistake, not only were they far too tight to enable strumming and signing or easy removal, but they had no fly. God knows what occurred in that toilet when he went for his customary pre-gig nervous pee but the rest of the group were two thirds into the set list before he reappeared. We also had Scottish songs to match the Scottish costumes which was an amazing piece of luck. We've also played at Irish themed gigs with the same good fortune. Welsh gigs though proved more of a challenge since 'Delilah' is as close as we get to Welsh although Strummers are never afraid to don a daffodil or leek or two. We can do Gosport themed gigs where we try to convince the local audience of the Gosport connection to every song we play.

Did you know that Elvis once came to Gosport?

- on the Ferry?

Here's a song about Gosport people

- 'Urban Spaceman'.

A song by someone killed in a Gosport plane crash - 'Buddy Holly'.

A song about the last train ever to come to Gosport – 'Chattanooga Choo Choo'.

Did you know that Gosport is the largest town in England without a railway station?   Sad but true, the local station closed years ago, and there's no train line into the Gosport peninsular which is outrageous, and not only the cause of the horrendous traffic congestion we must endure, but also another reason for the Strummers' success.   No one can get out of Gosport because the roads are clogged so their only option for live entertainment is the resident uke group. This is also a reason why we only accept gigs within the local post code area.   Elderly Strummers will not tolerate sitting in traffic jams, they are far too busy to waste time, and who would want to go to Southampton anyway.

Many of our venues weren't big enough for us. We were outgrowing the local care home scene and looking back should have been looking at the stadium circuit. In 2016, many of the big venues must have had vacancies since so many big names had sadly passed away in this awful year. We should, on reflection, have used this as an opportunity to push on and try to fill Wembley. We could have made it big, but always practical, we had another solution. If the venue wasn't big enough for the whole group, some of us would sit with the audience – we were very good at blending in with the residents since most of us weren't too far from being a resident. At many small venues, the residents had to sit almost with the band. On one poignant occasion, a female resident took a fancy to one of the better-looking Strummers (own teeth and still most of his own hair) and part way through the performance, started to tug on his trouser leg. The Strummer carried on playing but looking down saw that the lady had moved a little closer and was tugging even harder at his trousers and looking up with a grin on her face at the increasingly uncomfortable strummer. On subsequent occasions at this venue, the same thing happened every time. A year or so later, we were playing at a different place, and the trouser tugging re-occurred. It was the same lady.

Many of us thought that the Strummer in question could have done more. Yes, he was happily married but this poor lady had needs and ambitions. Surely giving her a little private attention wouldn't have hurt. She may have been very wealthy, she may have been looking to replace a lost son or she could have been looking for the chair of the escape committee, who knows. We like to think that this lady was our first ever groupie and had obviously moved care homes to see more of us. However, the reality was that she had been forced to move when her previous home had closed, another innocent victim of 'Austerity George and Dave'.

We had many discussions (some may say arguments) in the early days. One of the first and most serious was on the topic of 'shaky, rattley things'. Iniquitous little objects these, and apparently, the subject of many Ph.D. thesis. One of our troop took great pleasure in handing out to the audience from a large Tesco bag, tambourines, jingle bells, maracas, and anything else that could be shaken or rattled. The aim being audience participation and some measure of occupational therapy. All very well and a super idea we initially thought. However, the sound made by 50 seniors banging away at these objects was akin to a Tsunami in a tin shed. Although great audience participation and good exercise for the elderly residents, it was not good for the beginner Strummers. We could keep in time with each other, only if the room was perfectly silent and we could stare at each other's strumming arms. Could we keep time with this cacophony of noise in front of us? Well no we couldn't but this wasn't the argument. The argument was about whether this mattered or not. Arguments tend to grow and complicate if not resolved. In this BBC driven liberal world of equal opportunities and self-worth some members of the group thought it demeaning to ask care home residents to shake and rattle. The lady with the Tesco bag took a huff and refused to bring out her shaky, rattley things ever again. Sad for the people in homes across the Gosport area, but a relief for the group since accounting for the shaky rattley things after a show was a nightmare. They may, or may not, have been demeaned, but I'm sure some of them purloined shaky rattley things back to their room lockers – good luck to them I say.

This got worse when our MC passed the remote microphone to a resident during a gig and the man in question would not give it back. He sang along at the top of his voice to every song, or he tried to sing - his timing and tuning was worse than even us Strummers. He was confused. Last week was Karaoke and no one stopped him crooning then. We didn't have the heart to cut the power but his singing led us all astray and all in different directions. Half the group forgot all that they had ever learned, others tried bravely to get in tune and in time with the man with the mike, who by now was very loud, and others stuck rigidly to the original timing and tune. The result was akin to a drunken pub sing-along and opposing football chants emanating from different ends of a football ground. Still he had a great time, best Karaoke he'd ever been to apparently.

Growing older gracefully is a noble aspiration, but not for the Strummers. Making a fool of oneself gets so much easier as one gets older. It's amazing that playing to the smallest of audiences can bring out the Robbie Williams even in the quietest of individuals. It's also a little worrying how eager some members of the Strummers are to dress up and make a fool of themselves. Some of course will always value their social status and dignity and for some acting the fool is a step too far. I have cried with joy and laughter stood alongside members of the group dressed in long black wigs and *singing 'Tiptoe Through the Tulips'* in a Tiny Tim falsetto screech. Or our Scottish singer donning a tartan hat the size of a dustbin lid during *'Donald Where's your Troosers'* or a lone Strummer wearing a bra and suspenders for *'The Lumberjack Song'* – that's what I call entertainment! Or a Strummer donning idiotic specs during every Buddy Holly song, much to the amusement of the audience but less so the Strummers since previously mentioned Strummer obviously couldn't see to strum with the blanked-out glasses on. I've lost count of the silly hats donned by Strummers over the years especially at Christmas. Still this gave lots of opportunity for one of my favourite one liners....

That hat suits you – it looks ridiculous!

These events were all unplanned and came as much as shock to the Strummers as the audience – what fun!

61

Chapter Six – Facing the Audience

In all these years, I've never seen the Strummers. It's an unresolvable conundrum. You can't be in it and be in the audience simultaneously. Some have tried. We had one outdoor gig when members of the group took it in turns to witness the group from an audience perspective. This was fine when turns were taken. However, as the set progressed, Strummers got too excited and more were leaving than staying. The sound was getting weaker and weaker by the minute. It was therefore no great surprise when they reported back that the volume was too low! One day we should buy a mirror and put it on the practice room wall so we could watch ourselves. Although this probably wouldn't work since we still have Strummers who have never seen the audience never mind themselves. The only eye contact is with their music sheets. Bifocals pre-programmed by Specsavers to focus on nothing else but the music sheet. Strummers daren't look up. If they look away from the music sheet they'll never find their place again – despite the fact we've played these bloody songs a thousand times. Looking up and facing the audience is still a skill to be nailed.

A similar thing happened whenever we played rock and roll. Our best singer and loudest strummer couldn't resist charming the ladies in the audience by rushing out to drag them up to dance. Someone should produce a list of things that you can't do when playing a uke (I think I'll start a Tweet on this) and spinning old ladies into a jive frenzy is one of them. I still remember the disappointment this caused, not only for our singer but also for the poor ladies. Without our best singer, our sound lessened, we lost the Rock in our Roll, and even the best of the Strictly Come Dancing professionals would have found jiving to our pathetic output impossible.   The sad sight of a disappointed senior been left without partner, her big chance lost as we grabbed our man back into the fold to re pump our volume.

The Strummers have avoided most social media and most post 1960's technology.   In a Strummers mind, Twitter and Tinder remain characters in Dandy or Beano. Spotify is a game played on long car journeys to keep the grandchildren amused. However digital photography has taken off in the strumming generation, probably because it's cheap and easy. Our audiences love to take lots of pictures which is very strange, maybe it's the lure of our blue and beige uniforms. Fortunately, no one has yet asked a Strummer for a selfie. I dread to think of the repercussions of any such a request since I have vague recollections of a selfie being something very different when I was a boy scout. The blue and beige pulls in the snappers and we have lots of images of the band performing. Pictures from early gigs clearly show about twenty Strummers strumming through a blur of blue and beige. The tops of twenty heads are clear and visible, but no faces. It may be that some Strummers were non-dom tax exiles moonlighting and on the run from HRMC or the Benefits Police and therefore couldn't risk recognition. Maybe they couldn't face being pictured in a care home since many Strummers are a little too close to the day when they may have no choice. Maybe we were a little afraid of the audience so chose the traditional English thing of avoiding all eye contact at any cost. The truth is that all Strummers were, and some still are, totally fixated on their music sheets and daren't risk taking an eye off the sheet even for one nano second, making audience eye contact impossible. Take away the music sheets and we would get eye contact but no music.

Strummers have tried and failed to learn songs by heart. Ageing grey matter and years of abuse has taken its toll and the average Strummer's brain can barely remember when the next gig is, never mind committing a whole song to memory. Asked to play a song from memory and the hardiest Strummers may manage, just, Sloop John B, but only because this is probably our most played song over the years – and it's relatively easy. Tutors are always telling us to look up, smile, interact, and face the punters. Strummers are learning to take a glimpse at the sheet, maybe once per line and then look up and strum on, but it's slow painful progress. Truth is looking at and engaging with the audience is far more important than perfect chord strumming. I know of several occasions when a Strummer has strummed through a whole song using the wrong song chords and did anyone notice?

Another law is that anything written on the song sheet must be obeyed. One Strummer decided to put the strumming pattern at the top of every sheet in a vain attempt to get all Strummers strumming the same pattern in the same rhythm. Song sheets appeared with 'D-D-D-D'. Four Down strums, easy, but one Strummer misconstrued this and continued to play the whole song using the chord 'D'. God knows what he did when we progressed to D-U-D-U! Is there a 'U' chord on uke?

Between songs we all look up, mainly to see if the audience are still there, and this gives someone from the group a chance to present a human face to the audience. There's an ongoing debate in the group as to who should be the MC of the gigs. One member is superb at getting the audience going. Cheery-cheer-leader is excellent as the shouting, cheering, clapping and arm waving MC. Like a demented frustrated over-enthusiastic PE teacher. Another, the Hypnotic History Man, must have been a frustrated music professor since each song is introduced with such historical accuracy and detail that the audiences began to think that they'd mistakenly drifted into an Open University seminar.

It's amazing how some get fixated on the deep meaning of songs. Remember all the fuss about LSD inferences in 'Lucy in the Sky with Diamonds 'or any Frankie Goes to Hollywood song. I remember when I was a young rebellious engineering student being forced to study something then known as 'General Studies'. This was a brave attempt by the College to move us students beyond engineering and broaden our minds. It was two hours a week of pandemonium and unadulterated lecturer bating. Why was it that the weakest lecturer was always allocated to General Studies? We students saw these periods as a great opportunity to practice cruel sports. I remember one such lecturer trying in vain to get our attention away from this weekly sporting event, and over the top of the abuse, noise, missile throwing and brawling he tried to get us to analyse the true meaning of '*Lucy in the Sky with Diamonds*'. A brave but futile effort – we loved the song but couldn't have cared less about its hidden meaning. He'd have been better bringing in some LSD and handing it around for us to try, but the Further Education system was not yet that advanced in the 1960s.

So why the Strummers thought that our audience would be interested is beyond me. Take that great Beach Boys classic '*Sloop John B*' for example. Cheery-cheer-leader MC would say something like "this is another song from our eclectic catalogue (no

68

one in the group, or the audience knew what eclectic meant by the way) and would follow with a tale about a ship full of drunkards sailing from a port called 'Eleuthera'. Only issue was that the MC didn't have the teeth to be able to say 'Eleuthera' and after 250 gigs no one has yet heard the correct pronunciation. Over exaggerated arm waves and slow claps would follow, often not wholly in time with the song.

On his turn, Hypnotic History Man MC would tell the full twenty-five-minute unabridged documentary of the Sloop John B, all crew names and details of their health and dental records would be included. It would have been quicker to recreate the voyage on the actual Sloop. In fact, it's rumoured that some poor audience members were overcome with sea-sickness and developed early symptoms of scurvy.

Then there's Frustrated Comedian MC whose pathetic attempts at humour raised a laugh or two in the audience, but this laughter was often drowned out by the groans of despair from the long-suffering group members. All great fun. Frustrated comedian MC would simple say that 'this is a song by a group from

69

Gosport... called the Beach Boys' or tell a tall story about why we do Beach Boy's songs. Its apparently because the Stokes Bay Strummers are also known as the 'Stokes Bay Surfers'. One look at the group would tell anyone that surfing, even the internet variety, is beyond attainable.

One potential MC, used only once, explained that 'my grandfather and me' is clearly a Shaman figure, a psychedelic guru in charge of the hero of the song. 'Nassau Town' is in an area of West Indian Voodoo ritual. 'Drinking all night, got into a fight' means taking LSD (usually administered dissolved in a liquid; resultant mental disruption and ego-death simulates a physical altercation of several hours' duration). The Cook who throws away all the grits and eats up all of the corn is the chemist who distils the hallucinogen; the grits/corn dichotomy is an allusion to the emotional confusion of the 'bad trip'. 'Hoist up the John B. sails...let me go home' refers to the wish for an unpleasant psychedelic experience to be over and done with. All too much, much better to just get on with the song.

Frustrated Comedian MC, wasn't fulfilled unless he had a witty link for every song. Not easy, and he often resorted to 'this is a song about Gosport' (which worked well for *'Walk on the Wild Side'* or *'Surfing USA'* or now for the 'stabbing song' – no, not another song about Gosport - its *'Delilah'*). At several Christmas concerts when introducing *'Let's Twist Again'* he told a sad and slightly distasteful story about how in his family at Christmas they always asked his 96-year-old mother-in-law round to play that iconic 1960's floor game called 'Twister'. This was already a disturbing thought but MC couldn't resist adding, that they always played it 'naked' in their house! Members of the group dreaded this story and grimaced as soon as it was apparent that he was going to tell it again, and praying that it would stop before the 'naked' punch-line. Desperate stuff and on many occasions the group pleaded with 'Frustrated Comedian' to find some proper jokes.

Vanity is a strange thing, not easy to analyse or identify. All our MCs are good. They all enjoy the buzz that being in control gives them. For those few minutes, they are probably enjoying a flush of vanity, but outside of that they are all nice people and not in the least vain. The group can't decide who is the best MC, and the Stokes Bay Strummers being a democracy, amicably take it by turn.

We've tried various wheezes to break up the gigs. We knew in the early days that audiences couldn't take much more than 30 minutes of 20 musically dyslexic seniors down-down-up-down bashing at 20 ukes. It would have been nice to have a little poetry or maybe even a cup of tea. But we are uke nuts, so any gap in the uke playing had to be bridged with a uke related filling. 'I know, we'll tell the audience a little about the ukes'. We are obsessed, they are here listening to us so they must also be obsessed. A great idea and on a few occasions, it worked very well. How much uke history the audience could stomach was the key question.

Hypnotic History Man MC – our Strummer not known for his brevity in anything, could talk, in detail for hours about the uke – yes, perfect man for the job. Well what do the rest of the Strummers do during this interlude? I've already mentioned our propensity for stray strumming. Strummers can't stop strumming and intermittent strums would ring out at any time. Frustrated Comedian MC and others would try and curtail the speaker by throwing out silly remarks – much to the amusement of the group and the audience. This man however, is un-distractible and once started he only had one version of the talk – the detailed version. The audience although a little glazed over, didn't seem to mind. They'd survived the constant harassment from Cheery cheer-leader MC to get them singing. They'd even survived the circulation of the shaky, rattley things and were already secretly working out how to hide their new tambourine 'gift' in their knitting bag. Wouldn't it have been great if they had simultaneously erupted into a cacophony of percussion, arms, and legs akimbo thrashing away at their new toys. Sadly, they never did and even this wouldn't have stopped our uke history talk. The only respite came when the speaker began to mention the different types of uke. We knew from experience that this singled the beginning of the end. By this time, the Strummers were in a stupor, a sort of uke driven psychedelic haze. A distant voice broke this spell, "soprano uke", "come on who's got a soprano", "ah Bryan – give us a strum Bryan". Remember, the Strummers can only play if they are 100per cent glued to their music sheets. Without music sheets their Ukuleles become redundant. We don't do ad-lib.

I still look with great fondness at our first ever group photograph taken on the beach at Stokes Bay. The photographer asked us to play something rather than pretending to play. We had our ukes, but not our music sheets or music stands, and the look of horror on half of the faces and the laughter on the other half, is captured perfectly in this photo (the photograph on the back cover). To be asked to ad-lib a demo strum was a step too far and caused some dramatic blood pressure rises among the group. We soon learned, and those likely to be called, spent hours and hours at home perfecting suitable riffs and licks – and then got very upset when they weren't called on at the next gig.

Stokes Bay Strummers are based on the beautiful south coast adjacent to the sparkling Solent. One would have thought that playing outdoors under summer skies in the tropical South Hampshire heat would be a real pleasure, not so. Playing such a tiny instrument outdoors is a nightmare. The delicate melodic sound gets carried away by the most innocent of breezes. We've had twenty or so Strummers bashing away with a totally bewildered unhearing unreceptive audience no more than 5 meters away.

Downwind, and you may hear something between gusts. We soon realized it was futile. However, we do not accept failure. There must be a solution. One member wisely suggested not accepting outdoor gigs, others looked to technology in the form of amplification.

On reflection, wiring up The Rolling Stones – 4 or 5 musicians, one singer – would be a breeze compared with 20 Strummers, 20 different ukuleles and 20 people singing – a roadie's nightmare. We had money in the pot so why not buy our own PA system? I recall seeing 10cc at the height of their popularity in the 1970s and being gob-smacked at the size of the lorries carrying their sound equipment. Over the years technology must have moved on and surely, we can find a PA system that would fit in someone's garage and the boot of a Ford Fiesta (the car of choice in Gosport). A couple of our technically literate Strummers therefore did some quick research and a 'System' with speakers which wouldn't have looked out of place at a Quo gig, a mixer and 4 ambient microphones was purchased. Eight hours were spent in a Strummers summer garden setting up the rig and labelling all the wires and components. We had the best labelled PA system on the gigging circuit, we had coloured and numbered sticky tape and labelled bags and boxes for each item. We hadn't a clue how to use it, but we were still pleased with our days' work.

Next outdoor gig, a local care home summer garden party, an ideal time to try out our new PA system. I can't over state just how much time and commitment some members of the Strummers put in. Three keen volunteers delivered the PA to the Care Home at 9 am ready for a 4 pm gig. Seven hours should be ample time to get it up and running. The rest of the group turned up at 3.30pm. The Strummers are never late. Each must get music sheets in order, unfold the dreaded music stand and tune his or her uke – fifteen times!

Most importantly, for this gig, they had to bag a place to stand, as far away from one of the fearsome microphones as possible. Why was it that at a previous committee meeting all had agreed to buy the PA system, but come the day 95 per cent were falling over each other to avoid it. A two-metre diameter exclusion zone appeared around each of the four mikes. Tearful shaking Strummers had to be coaxed to get within range of the microphones; and then be re-coaxed back after the initial feedback blast had shot them back two metres. Of course, we were not practiced at making music out of the inevitable shrill feedback. I'm sure that even Pete Townshend would have struggled had he used a soprano uke on Pin-ball wizard. We needed protection against the constant feedback, but could we still play if we were all wearing hard core industrial strength ear defenders?

Come on Strummers, you want the rock and roll lifestyle, step up make yourself heard. At 4 pm on the dot Chirpy MC began, using her own mini PA, she didn't trust the group PA and had bought her own. A wise decision on reflection. It may be that the audience heard our MC start the gig but we are not sure if they heard much else. The sound was louder, the PA was amplifying something. We were told later by a rare sane and sympathetic care worker that she thought that she could hear one or two people singing but couldn't hear any music. This we hoped was not critical observation in that she didn't wish to label our output as 'music'. Truth is the sound of the ukes was lost. The amplified sound of the few people singing close enough for a mike to pick it up was still blown away on the wind. To be fair it wouldn't have sounded too bad with just 3 or 4 playing and singing but 20 quiet ukes and 20 quiet voices into 4 mid-priced ambient mikes was never a good recipe.

What to do?   Some wanted to bin the whole system even though we had used a large chunk of our cash from the weekly subs fund to buy it. It must be fixed, we can sort this. In a desperate attempt to save face one leading proponent of the PA suggested that each of the 20 ukes needed linking to the PA as well as the 4 mikes. Our mixer had only 6 ports. A 20 or 30 port system would have been financially beyond our subs fund and would have needed Mike Oldfield or Rick Wakeman to balance the output for us, and at this time both were not members of the Strummers. Also, can you imagine the mayhem. Twenty or thirty wires criss-crossing between the music stands and unstable legs of 20 or more elderly Strummers.   Don't know about 'Health and Safety gone mad' it would have been akin to dangerous sports and we hadn't yet sorted out insurance since many of the Strummers were uninsurable.

Another Strummer thought he had a solution, apart from the growing opinion to ditch the PA and all outdoor gigs. The suggestion was to buy cheap clip on leads for each uke and then have a series of mini amplifiers among the group. Again, a wiring and health and safety nightmare, but we did try it. The leads were tacky and cheap and the sound from the mini amps was worse than cheap or tacky. Most gave up on this and realised that we needed to be unplugged. Acoustic was the way ahead. The Levellers were doing an unplugged tour so why not us. Some persevered for several gigs bringing along their own little mini amp. The result being that most of the band sounded sweet and acoustic but accompanied by what sounded like your mum washing up tin plates, with a tin scourer, wearing tin mittens, in a tin sink, in a tin kitchen, in a tin house or some such similar exaggeration. The death stares from the remainder of the group eventually got these amp diehards to refrain. Another member moonlighted from the Strummers by pushing his own cabaret act on the care home circuit and he had a different PA which he was keen to try and sell to the Strummers. Best thing would have been to sell our PA to him. Over the years, we have used the PA successfully to some extent; but it's at its best indoors for use in larger venues. It's also become 'a role' within the group – PA storage – and a member with a spare space in his double garage takes this vital role (obviously not a person living in the Gosport Post Code area - double garages have not yet been invented in Gosport).

It looks as though the Strummers are to remain a true unplugged band.   The only person allowed to be wired up (apart from Chirpy MC that is) is the bass player – ukulele bass - never guitar.   Even this causes hassle and we take it in turns to take the verbal grief from our bass player when no 13-amp socket can be found close enough for the bass amp lead. The mini amps still need to be dumped next time the local authority ordains to open the local recycling centre for more than 15 minutes every alternate Sunday, only during months beginning with A and on days of the week with no vowels – bloody austerity!

The group has been professionally wired on several occasions when we've managed to bag a slot on a festival line up or as warm-up for bigger local events, such as vintage car or power boat shows. At these gigs, we've thoroughly enjoyed the kudos and professional pleasure of being properly miked and mixed.   What could be better for the ego than standing on stage whilst a technician attaches a mike to the collar of your Stokes Bay Strummers polo shirt. Not so good when asked to say something or even sing to check the sound – terrifying for all involved.

Worse than even our own PA is the Fete's own amateur site-PA system. You know the ones, a mega-phone shaped speaker attached to a bendy flagpole, above a canvas gazebo and manned by the local jobs-worth in a felt hat. These systems are designed to make semi audible announcements to the whole site, such as 'the car parks full', 'HY13 XVC you've left our car windows open' or 'we have a lost child here – someone please claim it?'. They are not designed to transmit beautiful uke music across a vast windswept field in a September gale. However, we have fallen into this trap on several occasions. The organiser is always adamant that we don't need our own PA because 'they have an excellent system and we can use it'. Well we can use it, once the megalomaniac in the felt hat can be dragged away from the mike or when the raffle's finished. And then only to be interrupted between songs by lost children or car-park announcements. Not that this mattered technically, since the sound being squeezed through

81

horned speaker was no better than tinnitus. Many audience members were happy for the first time in their lives to have genuine tinnitus to drown out our transmissions.

We've had similar experiences at street festivals, playing among a line of market stalls, between a coffee shop and that man selling under-priced but over-loud country and western cassette tapes. Yes, cassette tapes of this genre are apparently still widely available across Hampshire.

We've also played in a Force-8 gale, on a windswept beach, alongside the Solent powerboat grand-prix. Noisy machines those powerboats. If anyone has the contact details of a sound technician who could have sorted out the sound for us on that day, then please get in touch. Maybe the sound engineer responsible for BBC period drama could help, since he or she has an unprecedented talent for muffling sound? I haven't heard the dialogue on a Sunday evening TV drama since that excellent 1980's Solent sailing soap 'Howard's Way'. Although to be fair this could be my hearing declining, and rather than join the NHS waiting list for hearing tests, I now use sub-titles for all BBC output. Maybe that's the solution for the Strummers, sub-titles for our gigs with an emoji uke icon skipping across a projected text. Great for a sing-a-long, no need for a PA, the sound would be irrelevant. On reflection, making our sound irrelevant may have some appeal, but eyesight and cataract issues would then become the predominant barrier for our audiences.

Chapter Seven – Practice makes Perfect?

Over the years, we have used several practice venues in addition to the fondly remembered Music Shop. The group was so keen in the early days that once a week wasn't enough to feed and satisfy the uke adrenalin. It was therefore suggested that we would improve quicker if we had one weekly session of tuition, and another extra session per week to practice and have some fun playing the ukes and singing. This 'learn/improve' or 'have fun' dichotomy still reverberates around the group – more of this later. One member lived in sheltered accommodation and she arranged for us to use the residents' lounge to meet every Tuesday for a couple of hours. This was a great venue and very apt as it turned out since we sat in typical high-backed older people's chairs with arms and *antimacassars all in a circle facing inwards to each other. Not much learning was done but we had lots of fun and laughter trying out songs such as *'Ghost Riders', 'Barbara Ann'* and *'These boots are made for walking'.*

*[*antimacassar – a piece of cloth put over the back of a chair to protect it from grease, dirt and headlice – vital if you're having Strummers round to your house but sadly unavailable since the 1940s and the demise of BHS]*

An issue did arise though. Our resident member was very keen to feed us all tea and biscuits, always adding that 'she liked a man with an appetite'. No one could take just one Jammy Dodger – it had to be at least three to satisfy our host. In fact, tea and biscuits sometimes appeared after the first song – hurrah the Dodgers are here - and lasted the whole evening. When one of our members became very ill in hospital every Strummer that visited took Jammy Dodgers in memory of this. On special occasions, she supplied Cream Soda. Do you remember Cream Soda from your childhood? Did it taste good to you as a child? Well, I can confirm that it tastes bloody awful as an adult and my stomach acid soon began to anticipate and dread those 'Cream Soda' breaks. There was no choice, our kindly host would stand over each Strummer until the last drop of the offensive, sweet, sickly, acidic liquid was drained. More surprisingly each Strummer would then lick their lips and say how much they loved Cream Soda.

We also took to playing and singing '*Jamaica Farewell*' at this stage, only to discover that one of the residents had said farewell to her daughter in Jamaica and found it too painful to hear that song. We would take it in turns to choose songs, and if anyone chose the Jamaica song we had to quickly check out the neighbouring rooms to make sure we were safe to play it. We did get this horribly wrong on one occasion when we hadn't realized that the lady in question was in the adjoining kitchen brewing our tea and stacking the dodgers. Eight bars into Jamaica Farewell she appeared, tray stacked to the gunnels but in obvious distress. Very sad, but also a little bit pleasing for us to learn even at this stage that we could bring an audience to tears – at least she'd recognised the song we were trying to play.

For some long-lost reason, it was this venue that we chose to record our first and so far, only CD. We appreciate that CDs are now old school and lots of our tracks have now been 'Streamed' - in the local river! Back in the day though it was the ambition of all rockers and rollers to burn a CD. We had to push on and get our music out there to our adoring fans. Thinking about it, do residents of Care Homes get spending money and would they have the financial means to purchase our CD?

One of our group had a son (yes someone in a ukulele group had been allowed to father a son – incredible) and although that son worked in a bank, he also owned a recording desk and all the wires and kit to string it together. Unbeknown to us the 'deal' with the venue was that we could use the lounge for meetings providing there were no more than 10 people. Maybe it was the diabetes taking hold from the Dodger abuse, but back then we were lucky to get half a dozen Strummers along to each meet. However, vanity kicked in again when it was made known that we were to record a CD and low and behold about twenty Strummers, or ten Strummers and ten 'air Strummers', turned up on the big night. Ukulele son was no doubt an excellent bank employee and no doubt very enthusiastic about his recoding equipment which was probably an un-solicited Christmas present from his frustrated rocker of a

87

father. It's probably fair to say that his record producing skills weren't yet at the George Martin or Phil Spector level, and to be fair he didn't have John Lennon, or any of the Beatles or even Diana Ross in the room that night – but he did have the earliest version of the Stokes Bay Strummers!

After what seemed like an age and the consumption of enough tea and Cream Soda to fill Gosport baths, and yes, you guessed, more Dodgers, we were ready to lay down some tunes. It had been decided to play 12 songs without a break. None of that multi tracking business. None of that layering of sound a la Spector – we needed more of a 'Jake Bug' approach. We wanted an honest sound, laid down so the listener is transported into a care home listening to us do our thing. Why is that the biggest mistakes don't become apparent until after the event?

About three weeks later, proud banker's dad pitched up with an armful of shiny new CDs. We should have realized from his look of apprehension that all was not at 'Abbey Road' level. We all rushed home that night ready to play our first CD to our lovely long suffering families. It would be a reward for them, a moment of sheer pride to hear and be witness to that first step toward a platinum disc

Our volunteer producer had made our first CD that much is unquestionable. The star, or should I say the only thing you could hear, on that CD was his dad. Intentionally or not, the only instrument audible was the twangy banjulele of his dad. Dad was an excellent player and who knows what went on between son and father to get that microphone so close to that banjulele and so far away from all the other ukes. To be among the nineteen lost Strummers on our first CD was a big disappointment, and apart from musical talent, it is probably one of the main reasons that this is still our first and only CD. It wasn't only the lack of instrumentation. The singing was bloody awful too – we'd never had the misfortune to hear ourselves before and the dirge emitting from our combined mouths was hard to listen to. To cap the CD experience, just as the final track is about to come to a perfect 'boom-boom' finish, our host can be heard saying 'anyone for tea and a Dodger!' Hopefully this alone will make the CD a collector's item in years to come. Vanity raised its head again and proud father actually sold some of these CDs, taking actual money from some of our adoring, doting and deluded audience.

On the down side the manager of the sheltered accommodation heard that more than 20 people were using the lounge, and that was the end of that residency. I've already mentioned that members of the group can become obsessed with the uke. Several months after the fateful CD recording a friend (not a member of the group) told me that he'd shared a car with a member of the group and unbelievably for the whole of a very long journey he'd played our CD to him - never again, he'll walk next time.

Gosport is not blessed with many music studios, although there is one excellent example and it is an employee of this studio who has become our teacher. Amazing, yes, we have a teacher – more of this later.

We have struggled to find practice venues since the sad demise of the ill-fated music shop. The financial means of the average retired state pension dependent strummer always limits our search. We've tried the obvious places. The local pub would be great but would the local drinkers be able to tolerate us and would the Strummers be able to avoid the bar since alcohol and strumming would probably be a stretch too far. In addition, do you know what they charge for a pint of weak flat ale in the pubs round here – outrageous! Reasonably priced alcohol is available at a local hotel which we've used and at the local football club which we've also used.

At these venues, the first half of the practice session was always dry. After a short toilet break, a couple of crafty beers, another slightly longer toilet break we would then reconvene for the second half of practice and then the magic occurred. The intros became less hesitant, the singing and strumming became louder, albeit a little less technically adept or tuneful and all songs, even ballads, ended in a resounding 'boom-boom' strum. Much more laughter, less vanity, no arguments, and lots of fun. The hotel was a superb practice venue. It wasn't that we sometimes had to share it with local tribute acts or wedding receptions, that killed it for us, but the price went up and we moved out. The local football club has a great team that is beginning to make progress toward the bigger leagues and generously offered us a weekly practice room and added the magic words – for free! We had practiced at a local Navy establishment in the Officers' Wardroom no less. We got in due to two of our members being employed there. A great plush venue, on the waterfront of Gosport and again with cheap alcohol. This came to end when that couple left the group. Probably not a bad thing since we totally failed to live up to the smart dress code demanded by the Officers' Mess rules. Some Strummers don't own a pair of trousers never mind a shirt and tie – and what exactly are court shoes?

A great venue over the years has been the local Guide Hut. Sorry, 'Guiding Centre'. The head Akela/angel/tawny owl, or whatever she's known as, gets upset if anyone refers to it as a Hut. The Strummers need 'Guiding' so it's the perfect place. The room is a step up from our usual practice venues. It's comfortable, warm, with lighting and it has a toilet, so we always get a good turnout. Another advantage is that the acoustics in the Hut, sorry Centre, are superb. Thus, we leave every Tuesday filled with pride about how good we sound and this allows us to blame the venue acoustics for any under-par gig

92

performance. The only disadvantage of the Guide Centre is the Guides. Strummers always turn up early for gigs and practice. Their enthusiasm and punctuality is legendary. Hark Angel doesn't like this, and we are always having to tell Strummers not to go in till the girls have left. True, the Strummers has some strange men among its ranks. The worst that could happen would be that some of the girls would get the full documentary about the origins of the Ukulele. I'm sure that all Strummers would pass a CRB check if required, but until government funding is made available for this it's probably best to succumb to Chief Guide's wishes and keep the Strummers apart from the girls.

Every Tuesday when we go into the Guide Centre there's a vintage tractor parked in the car park. There's no farms in Gosport, every field that ever existed is now either a jammed road or a cheap housing estate – there's no need for a tractor anywhere in Gosport. When we leave, the tractor has gone and no one has ever seen the tractor driver. Is it picking up a girl guide or dropping of a Strummer? Very strange. There's a Pizza Hut takeaway opposite the Guide Centre (health warning to Jeremy Hunt,

Minister for Health, not good to have Pizza Hut so close to Guide Hut) and maybe they employ a vintage tractor in a vain attempt to make pizza delivery more organic.

Another great mystery is that the exit to the car park is only one inch wider than the average car. A very skilled driver can exit without having to move the post. It is bordering on the impossible for the aged Specsavers card holding, Strummer, still pumping adrenalin after sixteen attempts at the strumming pattern for '*Whiskey in the Jar-O*', and in the dark and rain and probably still looking in vain for the phantom pizza delivering tractor. The mystery however, remains - one of the posts is easily removeable, its designed to be lifted out. We once attracted a strummer who was under 40 years of age and to this day he remains the only person with the sense to lift the post out.

It's amazing but every member of the group is uke obsessed. No matter how or when they started or what level of talent, proficiency or skill, each has become totally obsessed. All of them are Uke history and memorabilia buffs and all suffer from 'UAS'. Even if the NHS was to become properly funded this syndrome could not be treated. Don't bother trying to get a 'UAS' review appointment with a GP it would be a waste of the GP's valuable time. Appointments at our local surgery for even the most severe illness are only available with four weeks' notice of impending illness these days anyhow. UAS creeps up on unsuspecting individuals. It is usually suffered in secrecy and even family members are oblivious of its development until the symptoms finally appear. I'm told that golfers suffer from a related and very similar syndrome, which is doubly sad in the Strummers, since many of them are golfers too. Symptoms include selling perfectly good furniture to make more room in the house and in one sad case within the Strummers, having to buy a new house better situated to accommodate his developing illness. People with this illness need more support and it's very sad that in some instances even the partners of sufferers are not supportive to their ailing spouses. I'm sure that when a Strummer gets man-flu, or the female equivalent, that their spouses and partners are wholly supportive in administering the love and care required to bring the poorly individual back to full strumming health. I doubt many Strummer spouses are supportive or understanding of their loved ones UAS.

On a side note 'man or women flu' is never an excuse for a Strummer to miss a practice session or god forbid a gig. Much better to turn up and cough and sneeze over everyone, including the audience, to share the love around.

'UAS' is a real syndrome. Ukulele Acquisition Syndrome is rife among all uke nuts. In our group, every one of the Strummers has too many ukuleles - and one ukulele is one too many for some. The record within the group for uke ownership is nine. In addition, members were once satisfied with the thirty-five quid second hand eBay sourced bargain uke. Not any more, we are musicians now, we gig, we entertain and we 'must' spend more, we must have the Stradivarius uke. I sincerely hope that there is no such Uke, because if there is someone will turn up with one at next Tuesday's practice. Shoes with holes in, frayed shirt collars and hidden credit card bills are all symptoms of UAS. No human can play nine Ukes. Two may be acceptable, a traditional hardwood soprano or tenor, and dare I say it a Banjulele, would be a decent mix. However, Strummers across the country have a need to collect Ukes in every shape size and colour for some reason. A uke in the shape of an electric Fender Guitar, for God's sake why? I defy anyone to walk into a room full of ukes and not smile. Ukes are beautiful. Look back at those old pictures from the 1900s and note the fantastic designs, bright coloured art work and variety of shapes and sizes. The fact that they are under-sized and a touch ridiculous adds to the amusement. Couple this with twenty or more senior citizens in uniform playing ukes and singing, and the outcome can only be sheer joy.

Some Strummers have wall mounted their uke collection like the sets of flying ducks or swans popular in the terraced house of Lancashire in the 1950's. Other spend a fortune on elaborate stands to display their impressive collection of never played instruments to all visitors. Some must hurriedly clear away all the displayed ukes at the sound of approaching grandchildren. Grandchildren are only allowed to touch one of the ukes, a special uke purchased at the Oxfam shop for £5.99. We've taken this a step further recently. We not only hide the Ukes, but we also hide ourselves under the windows and ignore the constant door bell ringing till the grandchildren are taken home by their off-loading parents to wreck their own belongings.

A strummer is said to be in second stage UAS when (a) he or she stops playing and simply sits and stares at the uke collection, and/or (b) he progresses to UAAS. Ukulele Accessory Acquisition Syndrome. The Strummers as a group own enough straps, clips, mini amps, leads, bags, plectrums, music books, chord shape books, chord shape key fobs, DVDs, tuners, tuning books, fretboard guides, uke encyclopaedias, history of the uke guides, Bluetooth speakers, recorders, footpads, kazoos and shaky rattley things to fill a small bungalow. Great for the economy, bad for the Strummers' hard pressed household budget. Maybe when the group finally folds, the resulting

Southeby's auction of equipment will raise enough to end world poverty, or Gosport poverty at least.

Obsession has been taken a step further by some as they attempt to make ukuleles - happily combining their two main obsessions – shed and uke. Maybe this is an effort to try to reclaim the shed and make good use of some of that wood off-cut stack that's taken years to hoard. Making musical instruments, even tiny ukuleles is not easy. Luthiers are very skilled artisans with knowledge and access to the finest wood and the most precise machinery. The shed at the bottom of the garden, left over wood off-cuts from the mess that the local DIY superstore made when they last tried to refit your kitchen, and using a rusty chisel and antique tools is probably not ideal. Strummers have however produced playable ukes, cigar-box ukes and made several electronic ukes in various gaudy versions. One Strummer even opened his own on-line virtual uke-emporium, buying and selling, and making and selling ukes. He doesn't appear to keep a uke for more than three days and it's become a standing joke since every time he turns up with a new uke we all know that it will be available on the emporium tomorrow. Our first mentor at the long-gone Gosport Music Shop even took to trying to make

99

a uke and came in one week with the strangest looking bass uke ever to see the light of day. This was the start of the group playing on top of a bass beat in a vain effort to keep us in time. Suffice to say the Music Shop owner couldn't have afforded a readymade bass, even with the unwisely massive discounts he offered just before his business folded and he left the County.

I caught the making obsession after a clumsy Strummer knocked my favourite uke off a chair on to a concrete school playground. Don't ask why we were in a school playground. I needed to repair my pride and joy and being a careful Yorkshireman chose to do it myself rather than pay. I followed up this success when the heaviest Strummer in the band sat on a school sized chair, which duly collapsed under his weight during a frenzied Quo number. The chair was beyond repair (sorry County Council). His ukulele was in bits, which I successfully put back together. As good as new and he paid me for this service with bottles of wine. What a bonus - I was hooked.

First major project was a Stewmac mahogany soprano, imported in kit form from the USA at a cost that my wife has still to discover. Basically, an instruction book, a box of wood bits that needed final shaping, putting together and finishing. The big advantage being that the body sides come pre-bent. The kit came with a DVD and lots of YouTube links to previous sufferers. What was not clear was that to make this uke, one had to pre-manufacture several complex jigs to enable clamping and accurate assembly. I spent more than 10 times the estimated making time for the uke on the making of the jigs alone. If anyone wants a Stewmac uke I now have all the jigs you will need. A whole winter was spent in my freezing cold shed. On occasions, I had to scrape the ice of the inside of the shed window to transmit the internationally agreed hand and mouth signal for a cup of tea to my long-suffering wife, basking in the central heating indoors.

What emerged, after all this painstaking care, was in my humble opinion, a perfect, high quality and truly beautiful musical instrument. I was so proud of this gun-oiled masterpiece that I designed my own sound hole label and christened it Uke 1. I'd shaped all the pieces, made, and fitted purfling, fretted the board, formed the sound hole, added shell inlays and machine tuners. I'd used my precious jigs to assure perfect and rigid assembly. I'd finished it to a glossy mahogany oiled perfection and to my eternal relief and pleasure, it plays and sounds wonderful. Yes, it had taken me many hours and had cost about three times the cost of buying a readymade version. I will never own or play a genuine vintage Martin uke, but I've convinced myself that this little homemade beauty is almost as good. It is a sheer pleasure to own, play and cherish. So much so that I only ever play it in the safety of my home. I wouldn't risk it within half a mile of the afore mentioned clumsy Strummer or near the inmates of any care home. Sorry sons, but when you come to execute my last will and testament you will discover that 'uke1' is my most valuable possession – your inheritance sorted.

I have since, with my lovely wife, designed and managed the building of our new 'Grand Designs' house. I can honestly say that the buzz I got from making that first little uke and the thrill I get from playing it is on a par with the buzz from our house self-build adventure.

My next project involved learning to bend wood to form the uke body sides. I didn't want a kit, I needed to make a uke from scratch. I had four soprano ukes by this time so wanted a tenor – which sadly meant I couldn't utilize the jigs I had made for the soprano. More jigs had to be made, but in tenor sizes. Koa is the best wood in the world for ukulele making, so I imported pieces of Koa from the home of the uke, Hawaii, at great expense.

A uke needs two sides joined at the base and heel. I'd done my research and YouTube geeks from around the world made it clear that bending wood is a chancy business so I ordered enough Koa for six sides just in case. I haven't cried so much since I got the vet bill after he'd put down our old family dog. Bending wood into the shape of a ukulele is devilishly hard. I almost succumbed to a Canadian style triangular body, or even a square cigar box version. I spent the whole of a Christmas Eve in my steam filled shed, outside temperature minus 5 degrees trying to bend that bloody wood. I made iron bar ironing jigs and heated them with a gas torch to try and form the bends on the soaked and steamed ultra-expensive imported Koa pieces. On several occasions, I got to within a gnat's

103

whisker of perfection, only to try one last minute tweak and crack! Most of the Koa was disappearing, either thrown out of the open shed window or painfully smashed over my knee in frustration. Despite the sub-zero temperatures outside the shed window had to be wide open, it was akin to a Turkish steam bath, and I was in danger of suffocation. I've since learned that 3D printing is the future and on that day, I would have paid thousands for a 3D printer if it guaranteed perfectly shaped uke sides. In the meantime, could I get more Koa from Hawaii on a Christmas Eve?   Would my wife ever see the credit card bills?   Was I insane?   STOP – it's Christmas!

After another fulfilling peaceful Christmas in perfect harmony with my wife, children, grandchildren, in-laws and neighbours, I was more than ready to get back to the terror that is uke side bending. Fortunately, I found a local Luthier supplier who sold me some mahogany that looked a little bit like Koa and after 10 more rejects or broken bends, I had two acceptable bent sides.   The remainder of the manufacture was a breeze. My confidence was fully restored to a level sufficient to inlay the sound hole with imported abalone shell. 'Uke 2' was born. A two-tone almost Koa chunky tenor. Not my favourite uke, but full of memories and as I sit and play it, I recall the frustrations and the importance of perseverance in all good things. I still tell people its 100 per cent imported Hawaiian Koa and it looks great on a homemade stand in the corner of our new lounge - which of course has now been deemed an out-of-bounds area to my grandchildren.

At one Strummers' session, I met an ancient pony-tailed uke rocker who was playing the strangest shape old uke that I had ever seen and it sounded great. He had no idea where it came from. It was bashed and battered, the machine heads and nut were secured with elastic bands and he had to readjust the bridge constantly. He loved this uke and told me that it had been in his family for many generations. I asked if I could play it and it played like a dream. He wouldn't sell it to me, so the nearest I got was to take some pictures of it. I then did some research and discovered that the uke was one of a few still in existence made by Aladar de Vekey. De Vekey was reputedly a Hungarian Nobleman who, in the 1930's, somehow became a music shop owner in Bournemouth. Could this happen now in our post Brexit world you may ask

– probably sadly not. However back in the day his brand of Ukuleles, came in only 4 styles, with 1 being the least decorated and 4 the most. They are typically a Concert size, with an oversized body and a short fretboard that meets the body at the 10th fret (usually 12th or 14th on standard ukes). They have a reputation for being of very good quality. This was a very rare and valuable uke and I wanted one. My credit card was at uke- max, so the only option for me to become a De Vekey uke owner, was to make one. I had some history in Hungarian since I'd had to sing the Mary Hopkin song *'Those were the days my friend'* in a Hungarian accent ever since I'd told the group it was a Hungarian folk song. I'd already become a Uke magpie and collected many broken ukes, amputated fretboards and battered bodies. Could I make a Frankenstein De Vekey from the bits? I'd also discovered the pleasures of working with 1.5mm birch ply. The beauty of this is that it bends cold. No need for a steam sauna or a repeat of last winter's travails. The final product is admittedly a strange looking uke. It has a short fretboard (no worries since we Strummers never play any further down than fret 4) and a bulbous figure of eight shaped thin waisted body with an over-sized sound hole. It cost no more than £20 to complete, a genuine De Vekey is worth hundreds.   On its first outing, at the next Strummers practice night, I proudly displayed and strummed my creation.   Strummers took great delight in recognising the bits of their own discarded ukes. Our current tutor is a very talented musician, but more guitar-man, than uke-man, to be honest.   He took one look at my handiwork and said, 'why didn't you work out the correct sizes of the body and fretboard before you made it!'   What an uneducated slur. I admit that it's not my best creation and it doesn't come that close to De Vekey quality and this uke has spent much of its life at the back of our wardrobe – is it a 'swan' or an 'ugly duckling', or is it just too different to display to the uke world?

There's a very successful triangular body uke self-build kit, developed for use in Canadian schools and colleges. Interestingly the developers of this have rediscovered that the traditional mini guitar figure eight shape has little influence on the sound output or quality in such a small instrument. We can surmise therefore that shape is largely irrelevant and a square or triangular sound box can be just as good. If you look back at some of the crazy shapes of 1900s ukes it's easy to conclude that this was known long ago.

Maybe my next project will be a pineapple shaped uke?

All Strummers are expert on the history and origins of the uke but it's debatable just how much anyone needs or wants to know?   Where does this undersized, twangy little instrument come from? Apart from Gosport, thanks to the Stokes Bay Strummers, the Uke is most probably most associated with Hawaii - but why?

Many of the group longed to go to Hawaii and a few often wished that some members had gone to Hawaii for good.   If our weekly subs-fund had ever reached the right level, what could have been finer than a group trip to the land of ukulele. The ukulele's been in Hawaii for a long time, it's been in Hawaiian music since the island chain's independence and I'm sure that it will be associated with Hawaii for many more years to come.   If any member of the Maui Mashers, the Honolulu Strummers, or any ukulele group within hear shot of Waikiki beach would like to invite us over for a 'Jam – Strum' then let us know and we'll put the subs back up to £4 a week and start saving for the air tickets. We would be more than happy to join any 'Ukulele Lou' in a 'Yaaka Hula Hickey Golden Hula Dula' – anytime, just call!

We are a bit short of Ukulele Lous in Gosport and the closest we get to a Yaaka Hula Hickey Golden Hula Dula is the dance we do outside the ice cream parlour on the seafront just after the sea-breeze blows the ice-cream off the top of the cone.

Folklore suggests that the ukulele had its origins in the Machete de Braga, a small member of the guitar family brought to the Pacific by Portuguese immigrants in 1879. In fact, one of our Strummers still plays in the Machete style. Not because of some historical heritage, it's more that he likes the sound of a hard knife like plectrum slashing at the over taut strings of his plastic uke – each to his own!

Ukulele is still developing in Gosport but back in the day those native Hawaiians quickly developed a deep love for the instrument. So much so that they apparently coined the word "ukulele", or "jumping flea." An unfortunate name which when mentioned has caused some confusion and mild panic among our residential home audiences. We always claim that our fingers jump so quickly across the fret board that it looks like fleas jumping. A blatant lie since no Stokes Bay Strummer could move that quick and some don't even bother with the fretboard. An alternative derivation of the name ukulele is 'gift from afar' or 'travelling gift' which is probably safer to announce in the care home circuit.

The Portuguese may or may not have introduced the ukulele to Hawaii, but there's no doubt that it was the Stokes Bay Strummers who introduced the uke to Gosport. Hawaii and Gosport, two distant cultures that didn't merge fully until the Strummers had murdered the Hawaiian classic Christmas song 'Mele Kalikimaka' on four successive Christmases. The Uke became the national instrument of Hawaii in the late 1800s championed by the Hawaiian King Kalakaua. The King was apparently a total ukulele fanatic – and had he lived in the Gosport postal code area, and owned a set of warm winter clothes, he would undoubtedly have been a Stokes Bay Strummer. Instead he hired one of the original Portuguese immigrants to teach him how to play uke, and encouraged the use of the local Koa wood in its production.

It took the sad demise of Kalakaua for the ukulele to become fully embedded in Hawaiian culture. Hawaii's monarchy was abolished before the turn of the century, so someone was needed to champion the uke and good old Queen Liliuokalani (who wrote one of the most famous Hawaiian/uke tunes 'Aloha Oe' – note, still to be mastered by The Strummers) stepped up. Queen Liliuokalani was at the forefront of Hawaii's independence movement and therefore apparently got the chance to travel freely to mainland US of A. Obviously Pre-Trump travel ban. So, the lovely ukulele increased in popularity across the USA. Maybe it was the Hawaiian equivalent of the Stokes Bay Strummers that took advantage of the increased travel opportunities and embarked on a tour the States. It certainly wasn't us since sadly, the much-needed air service between Hawaii and Gosport was never established, in fact Gosport is the largest town in England without a rail station – travelling the six miles to Fareham is trauma enough, and Hawaii and New York remain distant dreams. However, The Stokes Bay Strummers were not needed since there was

111

hundreds of American uke groups by this time. A 1912 Broadway musical set in Hawaii included ukulele music and became a big international hit. The Hawaiian presentations at the 1915 San Francisco Expo included many ukulele performances and as someone wryly quoted at this time the ukulele is 'cheap, relatively easy, and vaguely exotic' so it's not surprising that the ukulele went down well in the USA. The ukulele started to move away from purely a Hawaiian novelty, to a USA novelty, before becoming one of the most novel things in Gosport.

The truth behind the mythology that surrounds the ukulele – where it got its name, the tuning and 'my dog has fleas' – is mostly lost to the Strummers. In fact, 'cheap, relatively easy and vaguely exotic' could describe Gosport or even the Stokes Bay Strummers. But how did the uke get to the UK and then on to Gosport?

The uke – in its louder, harsher banjulele form – started growing in popularity in music halls of the UK. The biggest star of the era was Wigan borne George

Formby whose banjulele strumming remains hypnotic and unattainable for most Strummers.

As it happens one of the Stokes Bay Strummers was born in Wigan, could this be the key? A banjulele in the wrong hands makes a bloody awful noise. Most Banjulele owners have sat in front of YouTube for hours reducing Formby's strumming pattern to an ultra-slow speed in an attempt to capture its essence. Slow the YouTube down, practice the strum at slow speed whilst keeping one eye on the YouTube action. Sounds bloody awful at slow speed. Speed it up gradually. Keep that wrist and hand flexible. Wind it up. Here we come George. I have it, I can do it, I can play like Formby! No, you can't – it still sounds like a twanging match in a biscuit tin. George Formby's syncopated, or double strumming pattern, is a joy to behold and he made it appear effortless. Hear a good player doing this strum and within a nano-second you will be transported back to Lancashire and good old George's 'turned out nice again' days. Most uke players have dabbled with the banjulele, those with any musical taste have put it on eBay and used the funds to pay the consultancy fees to repair their ear drum damage.

I'm sure we can agree that one poorly played banjulele sounds bad. Imagine six or seven? Yes, we in the Strummers have been infected. What instrument do you think you would play in the group if you were a little musically dyslexic? Or of you couldn't make the weekly practice sessions? Or you didn't have the latest music sheet because you are a computer illiterate? The sensible answer would be a nice quiet, mellow soprano uke with a soft felt plectrum. No such luck. Better to bash away at a banjulele with a head the size of a dustbin lid with a rock-hard super stiff plectrum. Multiply this by six or seven and throw it into a *'When I'm cleaning windows'* mash up and you have perfect disharmony. Those sensible Strummers, with their perky little sopranos can't be heard. No one can hear the famously witty George Formby words above the metallic din emanating from the cacophony of banjo bashers. Worse still, the Strummers always strum this song at double speed and this always ends with the group strumming like a barrel of frenzied piranhas as inevitably the speed of strumming reaches hypertension rate. In my later years, I've taken to making solid wood ukuleles, and back in the day I would have made one for free for each banjulele player in the group had they promised to burn their beloved banjuleles. I did think of asking Gosport Police several years ago, to hold a 'Banjulele Amnesty' – like the much-publicised gun and knife amnesties. Ashamed individuals could have handed in their offensive weapons for mass supervised safe destruction. I suppose however, that the police would probably think it more important to rid Gosport of knife and gun crime. I may threaten to withhold the police precept proportion of my council tax until they acknowledge the gravity of this problem.

Although in all seriousness the banjo-bashers in the group have added much to the mix. In my bias opinion (sorry banjulele players) Ukuleles should be made of solid wood – full stop. Not metal bed pans and stretched vellum and definitely not plastic. Many Christmases ago we presented all our younger nephews and nieces with plastic garishly coloured ukuleles in the hope of forming a family band. No such thing happened and I put this down to plastic. These ukes didn't look like real instruments - they didn't even look like real toys. The kids quickly began to use them as weapons and most were smashed by Boxing Day. A similar thing happened back in the 1950's when mass produced plastic ukuleles flooded the shops. Historical note, yes back in the 50's we had shops, you could buy things without the internet and credit cards. All you needed was money, and a stout pair of walking shoes – although both were in short supply in Gosport I'm told. However, the ukulele was mass sold to kids and the Maccaferri range of plastic ukes would have been Amazon's top seller had Amazon owned a shop in 1950. But after an initial boom and for no clear reason the Uke faltered in the 60's. Maybe it was the sight and sound of Tiny Tim murdering *'Tiptoe Through the Tulips'* but for the kids of Gosport, and most of the kids in the UK, the Uke wasn't cool. Not in the same way as The Spirograph, The Magic Robot, Hoola hoops or Slinkys were anyway.

The remainder of the century was dominated by traditional guitar bands and, as a reaction to this, the first decade of the 2000s saw a growing acoustic alternative scene using more eclectic sounds and more unusual instrumentation. The ukulele found its place in this sound. You may have noticed for example how many TV adverts include a uke playing sweet background melodies to soften the hard sell message. The sound of the uke makes people happy,

happy people are more likely to buy things – not daft these advertisers. Jason Mraz's 2008 single "I'm Yours" was the best-selling ukulele song of all time and a cause of conflict in the Strummers since it's still seen as too modern for us. Two huge trends that helped bring the ukulele back to popularity were the proliferation of the internet and the huge increase in imports from China and the East. Again, Gosport wasn't at the forefront of either of these movements. Broadband for some in Gosport still refers to an overweight all girl group. Gosport was the most pro-Brexit district in the country, maybe in recognition that we don't need the EU for our ukes - providing we have a trade deal with China. The internet has made ukulele music easy to access and has created a ground swell growth of people being inspired to pick up the instrument by others like themselves who are playing for their own enjoyment rather than superstardom – although we can still dream.

Apparently the first man on the moon, Neil Armstrong, loved to play the ukulele. Why then didn't he take it with him and play a tune on the moon. He had the perfect song - '*Walking on the Moon*' (I'm sure that Sting would have penned it a touch earlier for

NASA, had he been asked). This would have been, in my opinion, a massive step for mankind and so much better than swinging a golf club on the moon. He did try and atone for this, and after visiting the moon, he spent several weeks in quarantine, as scientists at the time feared he may have picked up strange bacteria while in space. He spent much of this time in quarantine strumming his uke. However, strumming alone is not good for the health, and had we known at the time we, the Stokes Bay Strummers, would have joined him in his quarantine pod, for a strum. Space bacteria holds no fears for us. Several of our members are in fact 'Space Cadets', this is evident by the blank eyed looks some have when we try to communicate gig addresses and pick-up times at group meetings. We also have a good number of Space Strummers i.e. Strummers who don't know the song or chords so strum enthusiastically in a space about 30mm above the strings – also known as air strumming. It may be more socially acceptable for some of our banjulele owners to actually play in Space. It's a shame that Hampshire's Major Tim Peake got the space station gig, since we could have nominated six or seven to go. This reminds me of that old joke - Can you play 'Far Away'?

Beatle George Harrison, before he passed away, collected hundreds of ukuleles, and was often pictured strumming or giving them away to friends. There is a Ukulele Orchestra of Great Britain that is hugely popular. They regularly perform worldwide to great critical acclaim. The ukulele business is booming and in recent years, ukulele manufacturers such as Kala have reported growth of 500-600 per cent ... and the Stokes Bay Strummers go from strength to strength.

Chapter Nine – Walking with Dinosaurs

We were, and still are, living the ukulele dream but finding a perfect balance for all is not easy. We are proud to accept anyone into the group no matter what their musical ability or skill level. This is important to us and more important than producing the perfect uke group or perfect gig. If you want that, then pay your money and go and see the excellent Ukulele Orchestra of Great Britain.

Retirement for some equates to a loss of status. When employed you had responsibilities, reasons to get out of bed every morning. No matter what your job, career, or profession it was this that gave you status. All of us when asked what we do – would reply with "builder", "accountant", "taxidermist" etc. We are mostly proud to be classified by our job and "I'm retired" doesn't quite cut it for some people but saying you are part of a ukulele band is a great conversation opener and it is this that has given a new and exciting identity to group members.

Volunteering in the community, becoming a school governor, taking up watercolour painting, pottery or joining a ukulele group, all help resurrect individual status and is therefore important to health and wellbeing. Being part of the Stokes Bay Strummers has become vital for many of the group in this respect. The group is providing a valuable service to the people within it and the undoubted uplift it gives and the happiness it brings, probably saves the NHS many pounds. Some people may have joined in attempt to replace or replicate their long gone professional status but most join for the sheer fun it brings.

The Stokes Bay Strummers are not perfect. Peace and harmony is not apparent in many community groups and the Stokes Bay Strummers are no different. Add to this the art and subjectivity of music and the pressure of performing and it's easy to see how differences of opinion occur. Differences arise in two broad areas, firstly, musical differences, usually around song choice, and secondly, organisational tensions. The group has up to thirty members. Trying to get thirty people to pull together

121

musically and organisationally can get a little fraught at times.

Finding the right balance musically is dependent on finding the right songs. Finding the right songs, to get a balance between making it enjoyable and accessible, and challenging to improve musically, is not easy. Achieving the right level of democracy over dictatorship, the right balance of fun and social aspects, alongside the need to be musically acceptable and professional in our concerts, all add to the internal debate within the group.

Song choice is a constant topic, not only the songs we play at gigs but also the songs we play for our own fun at group meetings. It's understood that people who choose to try and play the ukulele are probably not the most gifted musically. It's not as easy to understand how someone can have lived in the UK for more than 60 years and still not have heard popular Beatles or Stones songs. Knowledge of popular songs is not a pre-requirement to become a Strummer and the choices of songs offered up by some members of the group is wide, varied and at times very strange. Yes, Bohemian Rhapsody would be great, but not on the Uke, or not on our ukes at least. One younger (40-

ish) member quit the group because we couldn't get our head around a Stones medley he'd expertly put together. He left to form is own group and I haven't heard yet if the Stones medley turned out well for them.

We've had younger members, and some older members who wish sometimes to try modern songs. Not all our audiences are pensioners, we get families and children at gigs and something current would go down a treat. Ukulele is cool again and is widely used to provide background for many TV series and adverts. New songs by young artist featuring ukes have become very popular. Not so much in the Stokes Bay Strummers though where modern songs are sometimes attempted but never adopted. 'I'm Yours' by Jason Mraz and 'Hey Soul Sister' by Train are both great modern uke songs that despite trying never made it on to the Strummers set list. Instead the group mostly favour songs such as '*What do you want to make those eyes at me for*' or '*I'm into Something good*' – basically any 1950s or 60s hit. Strummers are never short of song suggestions from the past. We play songs from the West End or long forgotten black and white Hollywood musicals and to be fair many of our audiences appreciate us resurrecting these tunes. It also gives us scope to mimic whip-cracking noises (Deadwood Stage) and train noises (Chattanooga Choo Choo) which can only be a good thing.

On this matter, one Strummer bought back a genuine train whistle from a holiday in Chattanooga and one of our ladies took great delight in blowing it, not always at the right time (I hear that train a coming – now, now, blow it now!) but always with gusto. Sadly, that Strummer moved to a new house and had to leave the group so the whistle was lost. In response, a second Strummer went all the way to Chattanooga, Tennessee, USA to buy a replacement, only to discover that a week before someone had purchased the last train whistle in Chattanooga. The last whistle in Chattanooga, so sad, not least in terms of the financial discomfort caused by the cost of travelling to the USA, but also a clear lesson than internet shopping is best. The Strummer therefore turned up sheepishly at the next Strummers' practice session having failed in his mission and decided to keep quiet. However, at the exact correct moment in Chattanooga Choo there was a clear golden shrill of a genuine Chattanooga whistle emanating from the back of the group. How could this be? Had the deserting Strummer returned? Had someone in the group discovered how to shop on the internet? Had the 'Emporium' reopened by selling home made Chattanooga whistle imitations whittled from Fairy Liquid bottles? No, incredulously and unknowingly a third Strummer from our group had visited Chattanooga the week before and bought the last whistle. It remains a mystery why the train whistle shop owner in Chattanooga didn't say who had bought the last ever whistle, and why he isn't ordering more!

If you consider, and some Strummers do, that modern songs are those from the 1950s and 1960s then modern songs are the backbone of our repertoire. We love a 1960s song. Easy chords, melodic tune, repetitive, short, great rhythm, and simple lyrics – ideal. *'Barbara Ann', 'These Boots are made for Walking', 'I'm a believer'* – all sorted. We love a Buddy Holly, Elvis, or a Neil Diamond. Some songs from this golden era have proved unsuitable. Many of the Beatles songs for example use chords that are too tricky for many Strummers. Also, the Chuck Berry classic 'Johnny be Good', a great song if you play it on your own. Try singing it with twenty Strummers and the 'go-go-go-goes' take over. I have cried with laughing at practice sessions whilst we tried and failed to get the right number of go-go-goes! Go Johnny go!

We had lots of fun with the old Mary Hopkins song *'Those were the days (my friend)'* by not taking the song seriously at all. Not only singing in a mock Hungarian accent but also slowing it down, adding pauses whilst the audience anticipated the next single picked note and adding more 'Those were the Days' choruses after the audience had thought it was finished. All great fun but our music tutor hated it, and the professors of misery in the Strummers can't cope with the fun of taking the mick out of a song and producing our own take. We have to try and imitate to reproduce the original and our version of 'Those Were the Days' has therefore been quietly dropped from the set list much to the disgust of the fun Strummers. Funny songs work well providing the funny lyric can be heard over the strumming which is not always the case. We haven't yet had the support to finish a funny version of 'Speedy Gonzales' but I'm sure we could get some Mexicans in to help once the Trump wall is erected. No border walls in Gosport.

Our long musical middle era, 1970-2010, is largely unrepresented in our gig lists. Punk sadly passed us by. Despite courageous efforts, *'Anarchy in the UK', 'Ever fallen in Love', 'Teenage Kicks', 'My Perfect Cousin'* and *'I fought the law'* never made the cut. I for one regret this, what could be more entertaining than a bunch of senior citizens bashing out and head banging through a 'Pistols' number? Not to forget that some Punk fans are probably care-home residents by now (especially after all that head banging back in the day) and therefore are our standard audience.

Kylie and any 'Scott, Aitken and Waterman' output is obviously unacceptable for uke. We don't have the coordination for rap or reggae and Glam rock is never advisable in the Gosport suburbs. Disgraced pop stars from the 70's have been struck off our play list. Indie, grunge and grime are not, and never will be, on our menu.

I recall the day that David Bowie so sadly passed. In response, I quickly circulated a Bowie song (a uke version of Space Oddity – nothing too

127

challenging) in the vain hope of producing a Strummers Bowie tribute interlude. No such luck, and in the week of this momentous loss to music, we were practicing, would you believe the 'Deadwood Stage'. This was on the lesson plan, and even the passing of a musical mega super-star wasn't going to change it. When my all-time favourite, the great poet, song writer, singer and entertainer Leonard Cohen died I was tempted, but had second thoughts, to push out a uke version of 'Halleluiah' to the group. Halleluiah is one of the most recorded songs of all times and I'm sure we could have done a better job than that X-factor winner a few years ago, who practically murdered this great song. Had the Stokes Bay Strummers been around at the time of Elvis or Buddy Holly's demise, we would have been up and ready instantly with a tribute track. We'll never be able to respond to an artists' passing, since most of the artists on our play lists are long passed. 'We don't play anything by anyone alive', has sadly become our catch phrase.

Some would love us to play a grand musical piece, a 'uke symphony' to show the audience that we are musical, we are clever, we are cultured. The issue would however be that it would probably take two years (18 months arguing, 6 months practicing), to get it to a level fit for any audience and in this time 50 per cent of the members would have voted with their feet.

I have a terrible confession to make at this point. I love the song *'A Stairway to Heaven'*. What's so terrible about this you may ask. It's a great all time classic song, one of the very best, so be proud that you love it so much. The problem, a problem that has increased in severity due to recent events, is that it's not the Led Zeppelin version that captures me, it's the upbeat tongue in cheek comedy version produced by – Rolf Harris!

Back in the day in his tour of university student union events in the 1990s Rolf Harris had the young students in awe with his quirky version of this great song. What's more this version lends itself perfectly to Ukulele. Rolf Harris's fall from grace however means that the Strummers will never get to try this version. Sad but understandable since all Rolf Harris songs have become persona non-gratis. I also had a CD full of his songs and our Grandchildren grew up with them, so much so that when our 5-year-old started school he knew and loved lots of the songs. When his parents picked him up from school after his first day the teacher commented 'he's quite a Rolf Harris fan isn't he'. Our Grandson had been singing 'Jake the Peg' all day. At least he was happy in school, but we have since weaned him off and he's now more likely to sing inappropriate or explicit lyrics from 'Little Mix' or 'Justin Bieber'.

We are strummers not pluckers or pickers. Some in the group have picking ambitions. Some have ambitions to play further down the fretboard but these skills are better practiced in the safety of one's own home. Strummers like to stay in the zone of safety that is the first three, or at a push four frets. Strumming together sounds great, plucking together sound like the plinking plonking of a hail storm on a caravan roof. We have tried to pluck our way through classic instrumentals such as *'Apache'*, *'Greensleeves'* and *'Summertime Blues'*. If the right Strummers have turned up for the gig we can sometimes get away with it, but often a Strummer with ambitions beyond his talent joins in the plucking and the timing goes plinky-plonk. I still remember the look of horror when our first tutor demonstrated and tried to teach us the catchy picking riff for 'Brown Eyed Girl'. Some of us spent seven days in solitary confinement to master this classic only to turn up the following week to learn that our individual versions were all slightly out of kilter with the others.   Picking works well when played by only one or two of our more talented players but twenty or more pickers and pluckers of mixed talent – no thanks.

A good Stokes Bay Strummers song choice is melodic, upbeat, sing-along, good to play as a group and instantly recognisable not only to the group on its initial introduction but also to our audiences.   We've recently got better on the 'instantly recognisable' for the group issue.   A Strummer now brings along his iPad and Bluetooth speaker to practice sessions and can find and play a new song to the group before we start.   We can hear the proposed song before we murder it.   We then have the Roman thumbs up or thumbs down vote.   This mock democracy works to some extent but has resulted in the black-balling of most modern (post 2000) songs.   It's also encouraged a desire to try to perfectly recreate the original song recording.   We therefore can spend hours counting beats and listening to the song endlessly to get perfect intonation and harmony, when the truth is that 20 ukuleles will never ever be able to recreate the track and we don't want to be a tribute band.

Tribute events are very popular now and there are some great tribute bands. I saw one Tribute event advertised at a local adult only holiday venue that included Amy Winehouse, UB40 and Oasis – incredible that one person could do all this. The finale was one white man doing a tribute to Ray Charles, Stevie Wonder, and Daft Punk – I wish I'd had the time and money to attend. A ukulele tribute band doesn't yet exist since too few uke bands have achieved enough fame to warrant it. The fabulous Ukulele Orchestra of Great Britain deserve a tribute act and probably many community uke groups dream of doing this. Problem is the UOGB are supremely talented musicians, the Stokes Bay Strummers are something else.

It's an obvious truth that a ukulele band can never recreate a perfect copy of any pop song, unless of course that pop song is made by a ukulele band. Despite this, the Strummers still spend hours trying to recreate a 'track'. This is evident when a track includes a 12-bar instrumental break featuring brass or any other melodic instruments. The group can only simply strum through this, which is a bit dull, and usually leads to re-joining problems when the singing starts again. It's not good for the ego to be the one and only group member to start singing 4 bars early with the remainder coming back in an embarrassing trickle over the next 4 bars. The Strummers can't be counting bars during the instrumental since they can't do it quietly and 1,2,3, and 4 doesn't work lyrically for any song. It's also very sad for the audience to witness adults who can't count in their heads without mouthing their lips and nodding their heads.

We need a support lifeline to keep us on track during instrumental breaks. By far our most popular answer to this is the good old Kazoo. Do you remember the old shiny toilet paper and greasy comb makeshift noise maker that your teacher confiscated from you in the 1960s? A Kazoo is the handy more hygienic plastic version of this. Kazoo is Marmite, love it or hate it. Our tutor loves music and hates Kazoo, we love both. I'll never forget the look of resignation on our tutor's face when a Strummer walked in with an old-fashioned sweet jar crammed full of plastic Kazoos and handed them around like sweeties to all the group. The remainder of that session fell apart. The tutor couldn't compete with the childish behaviour of the regressive seniors sat in front of him who couldn't resist blowing their new kazoos at every opportunity. I need to make it clear, the Ukulele is a real instrument, the Kazoo is not. We now have Kazoo aficionados in the group and these people take their Kazooing very seriously. A Kazoo played badly sounds awful, and let's be honest a Kazoo played well, sounds awful too. The sound of 20 kazoos together is reminiscent of a fight in a cattery. However, we've learned from experience that whenever we fill the air with that awful humming sound our audiences smile – and that's a good thing. Ukuleles make people smile, Kazoos make people smile so why wouldn't we do both. Some Strummers would have a Kazoo interlude in

134

every song, but our tutor still resists as much as he can and rations the Kazooing.

Strummers can't sing if they have a Kazoo in their mouths and this may be a positive thing. However, the changeover from singing (and strumming) to kazooing can be fraught. Most Strummers have their Kazoo on a string around their necks and need to be ultra-quick in getting it to their mouth at the right time in the song without breaking the strumming rhythm. An almost impossible task and very funny to witness from within the group. A solution would be a Bob Dylan like wire frame to keep the Kazoo permanently about an inch from the mouth. However, this would be too much temptation and stray hums, toots and buzzes would surely begin to creep into the songs – we could very easily become the Stokes Bay Kazooers.

A more upmarket version of the Kazoo, and sounding marginally better in the right hands, is a melodica. This small keyboard is played like a piano with the power supplied by the operator blowing in to one end of it. We've allowed melodica on several songs. Our most popular melodica piece is the introduction to Neil Diamond's classic, Sweet Caroline.

135

Our melodica player has been trying to perfect this for 5 years and the rest of the group have been trying to dissuade him for the same amount of time. Either he doesn't get it out of his enormous gig bag quickly enough and we've set off without him, or the keys stick, or he hasn't the puff to transmit the required sound volume – but always funny and appreciated by the audience. We've had good mouthorgan players in the group too and this works well with the ukes. But, the essential point is that we are a ukulele band...... with a smattering of Kazoo!

No guitars, or those 'Guitaralelles' – six string crosses between a uke and a small guitar. If it's got six strings, then it's not in our band. The Strummers don't mind what the uke looks like, so long as it is a uke. Checked, pink, solid, Koa, mahogany, plastic, cigar box, fender shaped, triangular or pineapple shaped; it doesn't matter providing it's got 4 strings tuned to GCEA. Some rich members of the band have purchased 8 string ukes. Twice the strings, twice the volume, seems to be the only outcome which is fine if they can play well, but twice the volume is not always good.

We always have a totally dedicated, but frustrated, bass electric uke player to keep us in time. This doesn't always work and Mrs Bass gets a touch emotional (code for bites people's heads off) at times when the group doesn't follow her bass beat. We have tried percussion but mainly in the form of shaky rattley things. We used to have a washboard player, but he often had a bad thumb and couldn't play. It's also a fact that one can't play uke and washboard simultaneously and bashing a washboard for two hours was not an attractive proposition, so he took the huff and walked. No one knows what became of the washboard but let's hope that it is being put to good use in the depths of Gosport where electric washing machines are still seen as new-fangled.

It would be great to have some percussion to keep us in time. Another uke group nearby organises itself around a Cajon. I covet this organisation. I am so envious of their sit on box drum (Cajon – pronunciation ka-hon, a box-shaped percussion instrument originally from Peru, played by slapping the front or rear faces, generally thin plywood, with the hands, fingers). The band members gather around the centrally seated Cajon player and he becomes the focal point, the energy and vigour of the group. Another reason for my envy is that this group also play modern upbeat songs driven by the percussion. There's no way I would join this group however since due to stupid football tribalism, people from where I live don't often venture into their territory. However, been a practical and skilled man the solution is obvious – make a Cajon for the Strummers.

A Cajon is a good quality box with a sound board face and internal fixed drum brushes. It's not difficult to make but it must be strong enough to take the weight of an average strummer. Five more days in the shed and a perfect Cajon emerged. Made for less than twenty quid, and sounding great, now back to YouTube to learn how to play it. Here I discovered a beautiful bikini clad Latin-American Cajon player sat on her drum leaning slightly forward into her internet camera (and into my heart) to demonstrate Cajon percussion styles. I was transfixed, totally sold, forget the ukulele I'd fallen in love with a Latino Cajon player and I wanted to be her. After two weeks of initial bliss the novelty began to wear off. Beating out a basic 1,2,3 and 4 beat is simple but trying to add infill and interest is very difficult. In addition, two weeks of sitting atop this box and leaning forward to hit the drum face was playing havoc with my back, kidneys and acid reflux. I did try putting a small cushion on the top but amazingly this badly affected the sound output. Latino didn't need a cushion, no, to play the Cajon you need to be younger and fitter than I. My wife was also getting very fed up of the noise and to be honest I think she was becoming a little bit jealous of the Latino girl since I'd got her on continuous shuffle play on the new 50-inch flat screen. The final straw came when I decided to try the Cajon at a gig and 2 bars into the first song our bass player turned around and gave me one of her infamous death stares. Was I treading on her beat or was I rubbish? Whichever, I yearned to get back to my Soprano Uke.

I offered all the Strummers the chance to become the Cajon player and some did try. The main limitation was health and safety since the maximum load of the Cajon seat was probably about 15 stone and some Strummers exceeded this by far. Fortunately, we had a Strummer who was light enough and moonlighted in a different band and she was more than happy to take the Cajon. She only tried to play it on one Strummers' occasion and got a double death stare from the bass player and the Cajon hasn't been seen since. Truth is that Cajon playing is not just about sitting on a box and banging it, it is very skilled. So, until we can afford to import the YouTube Latino girl we will just have to wait for the Gosport equivalent to turn up – this could be a long wait. I would add that if the Latino Cajon player did ever agree to come to Gosport, or if any existing strummer volunteered to wear a bikini, I would happily lock myself back in the shed to make another Cajon.

We've also on occasions banged a two-foot diameter Irish Bodhran. Not to supply percussive beat but to deliver bangs. Great for Dave Clarke's 'and I'm Feeling Glad All Over – BOOM! BOOM! A great idea spoiled by our over enthusiastic amateur Bodhran player swinging a wide rotating fist to beat the hell out of the poor instrument. I recall with great amusement the surprise and shock on the faces of the band (and the audience) whenever these two over loud booms rang out. Not very Irish, not at all good for the band's hearing and to be honest not worth the effort of lugging the bodhran to the gigs. However, this song supplied the perfect vehicle for frustrated comedian MC to ask in true Ken Dodd style, 'is there anyone in the audience called Glad?' and yes, you guessed, adding 'Do you feel Glad all over?'

A constant topic of debate in uke circles is fingers or plectrum. It is argued that strumming with thumb and fingers allows more versatility and variety. Strumming with a plectrum is usually louder and can be good for picking. In the Strummers, we allow and neither encourage or discourage either. A plectrum can be a great comfort at gigs, it helps the volume and being less fussy than fingers helps the confidence. I have heard of UK ukulele groups that ban plectrum use totally and if the group leader detects a click of a plectrum on a uke string he has the offending person removed - a bit totalitarian for the Strummers, it's Gosport not North Korea.

We are more refined in the Strummers and the main topic of debate is type of plectrum, or to be more precise what material the plectrum should be made from. Most Strummers agree that a hard-plastic guitar type plectrum is unsuitable for uke. However, we still have Strummers who insist and persist and the resulting sound is not good, akin to a mass tiddlywink contest in an echo chamber or a fight in a scythe factory. The democracy that is the Stokes Bay

141

Strummers however, prefers to cajole and encourage rather than dictate. Thus, the offending plectrums keep re appearing. Why can't they hear the awful noise they are making?

I managed to get hold of some leather off-cuts from the most prestigious car manufacturer in the world, the material that the most prestigious car manufacturer in the world makes the most prestigious leather car seats in the world. Dark red and cream high quality thick sumptuous leather. What was I to so with it? My wife had a mind to get me to reupholster the ottoman at the bottom of our bed. However, I didn't know what an Ottoman was, so that was quickly discounted. This leather was special it had to be used for a special purpose. Would a leather Ukulele work? Probably not. Leather plectrums though – a brilliant idea – and Rolls Royce plectrums even better, no one would refuse to use these, plastic plectrums gone forever. It's amazing how many plectrums can be made from even the smallest leather off-cut. I had enough leather to supply the whole uke world had I had the inclination, but these were special and reserved for the best uke band in the world – the Stokes Bay Strummers. I made about 50 dual cream and dark red Rolls Royce plectrums and took great pride in giving then out to the group. The plectrums were perfect and many Strummers are still using them today. I may have to buy a Rolls Royce just to cut up the seats to make another batch. Some of the plectrum criminals have however reverted and the harsh plastic clicking has returned. Maybe we need the North Korean Plectrum Police to carry out a raid at the Guide Hut to compulsory decommission all hard plectrums by dissolving them in acid. Come to think of it the hard plectrum users also play the cheapest tinniest ukes and the acid could also help in this respect.

Chapter Eleven – On the road!

On the road – not any road, only those within the 'PO' post code!

Amazingly the Stokes Bay Strummers have now played more than 250 gigs and the group is just as enthusiastic as ever. All the gig money collected goes directly to our chosen annual charity, and group members sew all their own sequins and pay their own expenses. The bread and butter gig is usually local and usually to a mature audience either through a club, something like the WI or a local charity. Audience size between 25 and 100.

So, what does a Stokes Bay Strummers gig look, sound and feel like?

Strummers always look the part in either of the two uniforms. Strummers are always well turned out. Jeremy Corbyn, if he does play uke, would have to accept our dress code if he wanted to join. For day-time gigs it's a light blue polo with Strummers logo accompanied by beige trousers. Beige is an age thing and the phrase that 'life is too short to wear beige', hasn't reached the Strummers yet. Light blue silk waistcoats, black or white shirt, blue bow tie and black trousers are for night time and upmarket gigs – yes, the Strummers have played at some posh events including weddings and corporate dinners.

Strummers always turn up early. It may be nervous tension, or the fact that most of them have nothing else better to do, but the band will be ready to play a good thirty minutes before strum-off time. This usually means that the whole group is stood in position strumming arms poised like coiled springs, 20 nervous faces staring at the audience for 30 minutes. No one ever knows who's going to turn up. The diary system of putting your name in a book remains too high tech and complicated for some, so it's always a surprise to learn that there's enough Strummers to go on.

The group plays best when in a huddle. Far too often, for reasons unknown, the group assembles in two long straight rows. The result being that the distant left-hand end of the line ends up playing half a bar behind the right-hand end because they can't hear or see each other. The output from this is akin to school children singing conflicting rounds of 'London Bridge'. Ideally then it must be a horse shoe shaped line to enable the Strummers on the ends to hear and see all the other Strummers. Once a Strummer has plonked his or her music stand on his or her square foot of floor then it's almost impossible to move that Strummer. Despite calls to get closer there's always one or two who like to keep their distance and maintain a good three or four feet gap between themselves and the rest of the group – maybe they don't really like being in the group, or maybe they just want to play alone. Two lines, ladies seated on the front line and gentlemen standing behind. The bass player at one end, next to the only 13-amp socket in the room and the MC seated at the other end ready to jump out to lead the cheering and dancing. It's always advisable to place the poor singers and poorer players alongside better ones. This is obviously achieved surreptitiously so as not to upset anyone. Seating/standing plans have been tried but Strummers didn't like been told what to do and some would stand their ground like a seven-year-old throwing a tantrum rather than following an imposed plan.

As already mentioned each Strummer insists on using his or her own music and music stand. So, twenty Strummers equals twenty stands. This is usually disguised by matching Strummer blue antimacassars that slip over the front of each of the stands. The stage area therefore is very busy with twenty Strummers and twenty music stands. Add to this that some Strummers insist on bringing to stage; water bottles, comfort blankets, thermos and four ukes (one gets played and three remain unused on specially manufactured little stands). One Strummer has even manufactured his own wheeled pull along bag the size of a council wheelie bin, and this of course must remain nearby. The whole production is therefore a health and safety nightmare, even without the spaghetti wiring associated with the useless PA, it is amazing that someone hasn't been maimed. It only takes one Strummer unsteady on his or her feet for the whole thing to collapse like dominoes and the whole group would have to be transported to A&E together, since they'll be bound together by bent music stands and PA cords, to get fragments of expensive ukes removed from their body parts. An awful thought and thankfully this has been avoided so far, but one day!

147

Another health hazard is the 3m long banner, splendid in Strummer-Blue and purchased at great expense. This goes up when someone remembers to bring it along, and if someone is agile enough to put it up behind the group. So even before a note is sung or a chord strummed the group look the part, and remember the whole group has looked the part for 30 minutes and still haven't started, much to the confusion of the seated audience.

Our opening song is always 'I Hear Stokes Bay Strummers Strumming'. This is the only 'original' song in the set list and was penned by yours truly. Not such a great feat of song writing, more Needs Must than Neil Diamond but sung to the tune of 'Bad Moon Rising' it always gets gigs off to a rousing start. And has the added advantage of being very easy to sing and play, so a good warm up song. It goes like this...

I hear ukuleles strummin'

You'll see good times here today

I hear Stokes Bay Strummers strummin

We have good times down the Bay

So come on down the Bay,

come and hear us play

there's some strummin to be done

We need you all to sing together

Cos we don't practice every day

We play the ukes and we're not clever

But we see good times here today

So don't go out today stay and hear us play

There's some strummin to be done

So join with us today and sing as we play

there's some singing to be done

Here's the song again with the alternative truth sub-titles.

I hear ukuleles strummin'

[at last, we've waited all this time to get going, we can't hear - can you?]

You'll see good times here today

[we are having a good time – and so will you, or else]

I hear Stokes Bay Strummers strumming

[getting louder and almost in time by now]

We have good times down the Bay

[no one has ever had a good time down the Bay]

So come on down the Bay come and hear us play

[come on down!]

there's some strummin to be done

[its hard work – all this uke bashing]

We need you all to sing together

[cos we can't sing in tune]

Cos we don't practice every day

[we don't practice any day]

We play the ukes and we're not clever

[nothing could be truer]

But we see good times here today

[always optimistic]

So don't go out today stay and hear us play

[the doors are locked]

There's some strummin to be done

[we'll do the strumming, no one touches my uke]

So join with us today and sing as we play

[please we beg you, join in we need you]

there's some singing to be done

[sing, please sing, the gig's hopeless if you don't sing]

A Strummers' interloper did try to usurp this song by producing a version of 'Alexander's Rag Time Band' with the lyric 'We are the Stokes Bay Strummers Band' – obviously not in the same league and not taken up.

Songs are then an eclectic mix focusing on uke favourites such as, *Sloop John B, Rave on, Country Roads, I'm a Believer, Happy Together, Good Luck Charm, Under the Moon of Love, Chatanooga*

151

Choo, Sailing, I'll Tell Me Ma. Whiskey in the Jar, All my Loving, I saw her Standing There, Valerie, Glad All Over, Bye Bye Love, Hello Mary Lou, an Abba Medley etc etc.

There's now more than a hundred such songs to choose from and it's a key task in the group to produce set lists prior to each gig so that everyone (in theory) turns up practiced and with the right music sheets

The set always ends with a good old Rock and Roll medley which usually gets people on their feet. Amazing but true, ukes can rock and the Strummers can rock too. *'Delilah'* is saved for an encore – which is an arm waving party triumphal anthem to close any concert. Yes, we now get encores – amazing!

It isn't all care or residential homes and the Strummers will play anywhere for anyone who asks, truth is the group never says 'No'. The ladies of local Women's Institutes love the Strummers and the group has played some great gigs and had lots of fun with the good old WI and thankfully they have never asked us to join them in a uke rendition of 'Jerusalem'. Never been invited to a MI though. Is there such a thing? The University of the Third Age (U3A) is always a good audience, despite their obvious high intellect they still love to get involved and always have a good sing along. Although they can throw our MC by shouting out requests for songs. This can't happen, Strummers prepare a 'gig book' containing only the allotted songs. Even if someone asks for a song that the group has played a thousand times it couldn't be done without the safety net and prop of the music sheet. Remember how babies become attached to a cuddly toy or piece of soft material and can't sleep or function unless it is very close at hand – well this is how the Strummers feel about their song sheets and this may be another reason that they stare at them longingly rather than looking at the audience occasionally.

Living in a navy /MoD region the Strummers have done many gigs with a military link. One of the first real big gigs in a massive theatre with a paying audience was in HMS Sultan along with the Solent Singers. The Singers did a fantasy set in which they imagined a sunny afternoon being entertained by a ukulele band and surprise-surprise, we emerged from the foot lights to do that very thing – a triumph of stage production. The only down side was that the key jammed on the melodica in the intro to 'Sweet Caroline' and this flat fart of a note rather spoiled the sunny day vision, but the group strummed on stoically. The Strummers have sunk at the submarine museum and dived at the local diving museum where a whole weekend of pirate/sea related songs was required – a real challenge and the Strummers set compiler was only rescued by Ringo's *Yellow Submarine' and* Disney's *'Under the Sea'*. The Strummers have also been the pre-dinner entertainment at the Royal Navy's Submarine School Wardroom Officers Christmas Ball. No blue and beige here, the group were resplendent in bow ties and silk waistcoats and strummed whilst the officers and their ladies sipped G&Ts overlooking Portsmouth Harbour. The whole gig was akin to playing pre-dinner music on a sumptuous luxury liner. Wouldn't it be great for the Strummers if a residency could be secured with Cunard or P&O cruises? Free food, free booze, free holidays and a captive audience, not through locked doors as per the residential homes, but surely no one would jump overboard to escape the Strummers – would they? In fact, a couple of new Strummers joined the group after taking uke lessons on a Mediterranean cruise and there's a perfect job for a Strummer – giving uke lessons on a cruise liner.

Playing whilst people are eating is most off putting. Not only because no one can sing and eat at the same time but also because people don't pay attention when they are eating, which is a bit rude. The Strummers prefer a captive attentive audience that can join in and sing along with us. The Golf Club dinner is also a posh nosh do. The first half is 'quieter' songs whilst the golfers dine. This is not easy since the Strummers, like most uke groups, don't do 'quiet' and the closest thing is something like the Eagles ballad 'Lying Eyes' which goes on and on so fills up lots of the time nicely. Before the second post dinner set the golfers very kindly give the group free alcohol. As a direct result the second set goes down a storm. The counting in is at best erratic, the singing is slightly slurred but the inhibitions are no more, and the Strummers rock. Come to think of it the group wouldn't need any tutor and wouldn't have musical disagreements if we all drank more - is this the future?

We've also gone posh and played among the glass chandeliers and canapes at Southsea's poshest hotel for a confused looking bunch of business

155

delegates. Some tried to push for the country classic *'Crystal Chandeliers'* but some Strummers are allergic to country and western so it was dropped quicker than Del boy and Rodney's famous chandelier.

Unbelievably the Strummers have also played at wedding receptions which is great for the group, but one would have to question the future of any couple who books a 'free' ukulele band as the main entertainment on the biggest day of their lives. We've done lots of Tea Parties and are on first name terms with all the local clergy – probably because we are cheap. Our cheery MC made some large display cards with the words 'oohs' and 'ahs' and thrust them at the audience to get the audience to sing as our backing ensemble in *'Surfing USA'*. A great idea but we were playing at the local Macular Degeneration and Blind club so the effect was less than perfect.

The smallest gig we've played is at the local bakers which only has three small customer tables in a shop no bigger than 5m by 3m. Great when twenty Strummers cram in. The baker only wanted 4 Strummers but never slow to miss free cakes the whole group turned out to fill the shop leaving no room for an audience or any customers. Our gig booker doesn't like it when asked to limit our numbers. We are a democracy and whoever turns up, plays. It's every available Strummer or nothing. It's exciting and terrifying in equal measures not to know who is turning up for a gig. We have a gig website and gig diary book but it's beyond the wit of some to pencil their names into the book and looking up something on a website remains for some a futuristic pipedream. It's not that they have a busy life, it's more that some don't like being told to do anything, so ignore the book. I can't imagine the Travelling Wilburys having these problems but if you book the Strummers you could get twenty Strummers, it could be six, it could be ten who can't sing a note, it could be 8 who can't play anything more than a C chord – but somehow it always works even though it gets a little bit tense for the control freaks in the group.

We did have an infant school teacher in the Strummers which was great since he could control the disruptive ADHD elements within the group. He also got us several bookings in local schools. Great for the kids to get away from those awful screeching

157

recorders and witness some real music. The first set list we produced for an infant school gig was shredded. It's incredible how many of our songs were rejected. If one is being perfectly politically correct, so many songs are not suitable for children....

Jonny be Good – *degenerate and mentions 'Dunny Shack'*

Cotton Fields – *slavery*

Two Little Boys – *obviously inappropriate on so many levels!*

You're 16 – *paedophilia*

When I'm 64 – *ageist and no kid can possibly imagine someone so old, kids in Gosport have Grandmas aged less than half that age.*

Putting on the Style – *bad driving example and mentions Satan*

Wild Rover – *whiskey pushing*

Sweet Caroline – *too much 'touching me' 'touching you'*

Folsom Prison – *inappropriate since it mentions trains and no kid in Gosport has ever seen one*

Black Velvet Band – *'she meant the doing of him' don't think so*

Rocking all Over the World – *'going crazy' mental health discriminatio*n

I'm into Something Good – *obvious a stalking or drugs song*

Lying Eyes – *'she pulls away and leaves him with a smile, don't think so*

These Boots are Made for Walking – *mentions matches - fire hazard*

I'm a Believer – *religious bias*

Brown Eyed Girl – *racist*

Hi Ho Silver Lining – *'flies are in your pea soup baby' what's he on?*

Sloop JB – *drunkards and some hints of homosexuality*

Singing the Blues – *'the moon and stars no longer shine' - too upsetting*

Sixteen Tons – *not in metric units, and slavery*

Barbara Ann – *'tried Peggy Sue, tried Betty Lou tried Mary Lou' - not in my school*

Leaning on a Lamp – *loitering and stalking*

159

Drunken Sailor -*too close to home in a Naval town*

Eight Days a Week – *too confusing for the Maths curriculum*

Feeling Glad All Over – *not in school please and the only person in the school with any chance of being named Glad is likely to be the Head Teacher.*

I Wanna be Like You – *'king of the swingers' – too close to home due to Gosport's thriving swinging scene*

Urban Spaceman – *'I've got speed' – so has my dad!*

Pretty Flamingo – *hallucinatory*

Rave On – *what's a Rave Miss?*

Picture of You – *photography not allowed in school*

Lumberjack Song – *transvestite and mentions Bras (titter titter)*

We were left with *'Bring me Sunshine'* and *'You are my Sunshine'* and added *'Skin'* by the excellent Roy Bailey and *'I like Bananas – because they have no bones'* by ukulele Joe Brown – all went down a storm.

One of the best and most heart-warming gigs is at a remarkable local special school. This school takes children from age 5 to 19 with severe special educational, mental, and physical needs. These kids are brilliant and the excitement they generate as we prepare to play is fantastic. No inhibitions they join in every song and sing at the top of their voices – totally brilliant and exhilarating. Prior to playing the banana song we asked the kids if they like bananas and they all shouted 'yes'. We then said, 'we like bananas', 'do you know why?' and quickly added 'because they have no bones'. On hearing this, one very sweet little girl totally immobilised in a special wheel chair, burst into fits of joyous laughter. It was obviously the funniest joke she had ever heard. If frustrated comedian MC lives, quips and plays until he's 90 he will never ever get a better response and he should retire now in its glory. I will never forget the joy on that little girls face, a much-treasured Strummers moment.

There's always pressure within the Strummers as November approaches. Christmas is our busiest gigging time and settling on a Christmas set list is always a challenge. Some Strummers avoid attending practice on the first mention of the dreaded Christmas songs. Some Bah Humbugs in the group want a Christmas set list with no Christmas songs. One even

161

dons a black Bah Humbug hat for Christmas gigs and stands alongside the rest of the group who are splendidly decked in red Santa Hats and jingle bells.

'Why not give the audiences a good time and play lots of dance songs'

'What's the point of learning new songs just for a couple of weeks'

'Why not play what we are good at?'

'That would severely limit the choice - ah!'

'Christmas songs are all bloody awful'

'no more Shaking Stevens or

Noddy-Bloody Holder please'

'How about some modern Christmas songs?'

'OK do you know any'

'No'

'How about that Mariah Carey song

– All I want for Christmas, is you?'

'It's a dirge I'm not singing that'

'How about some carols?'

162

'No, carols sound crap on uke and

we sound like Songs of Praise rejects'

'We won't sing 'Hark the herald Angels' then

'Can we just forget Christmas'

… and every year we end up with the same Christmas set list. A 50/50 mix of what we like playing best, rock and roll and sixties classics, and a smattering of Christmas songs such as *'Jingle Bells', 'Rudolph', and 'Rocking around the Christmas Tree'.*

Every year we have the same discussions and even if we started practicing in July the Christmas songs would not be gig ready enough for some by December. Everyone, or everybody gets confused between *'Merry Christmas Everybody'* and *'Merry Christmas Everyone'.* After five years of trying the group has mastered the Hawaiian Christmas classic *'Mele Kalikimaka'* (Hawaii's way to say Merry Christmas). This is a real treat for the residents of Gosport in mid-December to hear about blues skies and palm trees swaying. Christmas is seldom green and bright in these parts. All we need now is to get

Bah Humbug to dress in a hoola-hoola skirt and we have the makings of entertainment. This year someone suggested *'Mary's Boy Child'*, not the Jonny Mathis classic, but the Bony M reggae classic. Now, only three Strummers from a band of twenty can maintain a reggae strum and unfortunately, we don't have anyone in the group of Caribbean decent (although we do have some with dreadlocks). The Strummers are renown for singing a song 'straight' and mock accents or intonation don't come easy. So, the reggae element of the song disappears and what we are left with is akin to a Primary School Choir singing 'Hark the Herald Angels Sing!'

However, despite all of this, it always comes good and I can honestly say that some of the best and most fun times we have had have been at Christmas gigs.

Chapter Twelve – David Cameron and

The Stokes Bay Strummers

The Stokes Bay Strummers are famous in these parts for two reasons. Bringing joy, fun and entertainment to hundreds of local people and raising thousands of pounds for local charities. This is not enough though. We joined a band. We long for the rock and roll life style. We want to be known for our musicality. We want a hit record (are they still called 'records?'). We want fame.

Perhaps we should apply for Britain's Got Talent (BGT) or X factor. Then, if we do well, in 5 years' time we'll get on 'I'm a Celebrity of Celebrity Big Brother' and make loads of money and become properly famous like those 'Made-in' stars (Made in Gosport – would be ten times more interesting than Made in Chelsea). BGT always has bunches of talentless older people doing stupid things, so why not us. We would need an emotional 'back-story' to get through the auditions though. Perhaps we could say that all the Strummers are asylum seekers who've come to love the Queen - God bless her. We may have to get a couple of Strummers to feign illness or disability which shouldn't be hard and we can encourage them to cry profusely on interview because they've recently lost their pet dog. Better still we could all bring dogs having trained them to bark and dance along to the ukes. Can't be any more difficult than training some Strummers to keep 4/4 time. We could even write a special uke song which praises the judges and their undoubted contribution to the country's talent pool (rather than their own bank balances). It could work. We could be the next (insert name here of any BGT winner if you can remember any - no cheating, Susan Boyle came second!)

Talking of formulaic TV designed by committee perhaps the BBC need to wake up to the Uke revolution. It's over-cooked and now sold 'Bake-Off'. In fact, we've had nothing but imitations of the Bake-Off formula for years now. We've had painters-off, even potters-off, we've had decorators and designers-off, the time is now ripe for 'Uke-Off'. There are hundreds of Uke bands in the UK. We could get that very pleasing young man from Country File to tour the UK searching for quirky uke groups. Maybe that nice young fella from 'The Choir', Gareth Malone could present it. He would need to 'tone down' the music theory a touch but he could maybe do for uke, what he's done for people who can't sing. We would have to go for blind auditions with spinning chairs propelling an over-tanned orange has-been, a beautiful younger lady, a musician no one has heard of, and a token American to maintain the TV quota for mumbled dialogue. Mumbled dialogue is apparently a priority now for all TV shows, apart from the adverts which must be transmitted at four times the safe audio volume – wouldn't want to miss that Sofa discount sale. We would then go back to judges houses for pool side strumming duels against the clock. The emergent uke groups would then go through with 'four-yeses' to the live shows at the O2 when masses of elderly people will be bused in, emptying every care home in the country. The rest of the population (those who know how to use a smart phone) would then vote using a vastly inflated premium phone number (terms and conditions apply). The winning group would be given a recording contract, a part in a new West End show written by some boy band has-been, and best of all release a record just in time to snatch the Christmas number one away from Sircliff, Sirnoddy or Sirshaky.

Saturday night TV sorted for the next ten years, sorry I think I've been uke dreaming again. 'Uke-off' sounds like a cough mixture or worse an order from an eastern European doctor with his hand pressed into a male groin. Anyway, probably couldn't get the Strummers to agree on song choice or what to wear for the auditions and the finality of four yeses would always be questioned by the Strummers since some would want three and maybe a maybe. Sadly, fame for us through TV must wait - but what about Radio?

We have local radio down here in the Solent. Chirpy chippy day time presenters relaying vital information about cats stuck in trees, inset days in schools (aka holidays organised to give teachers yet another break from obnoxious children), fallen trees and train line leaf issues. They also play music taken from the same genre and period (none of that modern rubbish) as the Stokes Bay Strummers. Surely, we could get on our local radio, but would that be enough to bring fame, does anyone listen to local radio?

We needed an angle, a back story, something to make us stand out. Thankfully on 20th June 2014 we got the angle. We were planning a charity event to raise money and food for the local food bank, and one of our members had the idea of contacting BBC Radio Solent to ask them to publicise the concert. An excellent radio producer at Solent must be a member of a uke group since he saw the benefits to the radio station immediately. Old people playing ukuleles for charity, ideal local radio fare. Not only would they publicise our gig they also invited us to play live on the bloody radio and to be interviewed – wow! In addition, and this is where the true fame came, we learned that David Cameron was booked to be on the same show. The BBC Radio Solent website had the banner headline *'The Katie Martin show - featuring Prime Minister David Cameron and the Stokes Bay Strummers'*.

Yes, difficult to believe now, but despite the coalition and the Brexit vote, David Cameron was our Prime Minister. On reflection, post-Brexit, he may now say that his greatest career achievement was appearing with the Stokes Bay Strummers which in my view is about right. I'm told that since that day whenever he meets chums from Eton or at his Gents' club he always tells people 'did you know, I once appeared with the Stokes Bay Strummers'. Of course, no one believes him, 'You'll be telling us you were Prime Minister next' – ah!

It was good news all-round for us Strummers. Not only were we to be part of the start of the downfall of David Cameron but we also had our chance for 15 minutes of fame. In addition, it was a blessing that we only had four days' notice prior to our radio appearance. Had we been given more notice we would have imploded. There was no opportunity to deter the poorer singers. If you were free on Friday afternoon you were in. There was no time to argue about what to play we had to pick our best and most playable songs. The choice was easy, *'Sloop John B'* which we'd been playing very well for years and something a bit more up to date. Our most up to date song is *'Valerie'* and we believed that this would work well on radio. No need to worry about what to wear, it's radio!

We did have to get to Southampton at rush hour on a Friday though and Strummers usually refuse to move from their settees during rush hour. Older people with all the time in the world will not take a 30-minute car journey if there's a danger of being delayed by 30 seconds, even though this excitement would give them a conversation topic for a month – have you seen the traffic on Newgate Lane, who designed that new roundabout, whoever, he must have been from Fareham. No worries, one of our members had access to a mini-bus, so to avoid any strays it was best to transport all the available Strummers together. They would have been too nervous to drive anyhow. So, after a couple of run through rehearsals we boarded the ICANGO mini bus to fame and fortune – and true to form we turned up at least an hour too early.

Radio Solent's Katie was a delight and put us all immediately at ease. Her producer (big time - we were being 'produced') was excellent and set us up in the live studio and we ran through our two songs. Yes, two songs, one more than the average superstar gets on the Jools Holland show. And, amazingly, even having heard our rehearsal performance, they agreed to put us on air live. What a buzz, when that red light came on and we began Sloop JB, all strumming in the same time on tempo and singing in tune. It was as

171

though the Beach Boys had moved to the Solent. After the deep bass, final twangs of *'I wanna go home'* rang out across the Solent airwaves, Katie the presenter asked someone to step forward to be interviewed about the group and the upcoming food bank concert. We British are renowned for our queuing politeness but that day we surpassed ourselves as everyone in the group tried to avoid being pushed forward to be interviewed. A reverse rugby scrum had formed protecting each other from the presenter's microphone. However, two or three Strummers were eventually squeezed out of the scrum and unceremoniously thrust at the unsuspecting presenter. The interviews went well, mainly due to the skill and tact of the well-trained presenter and we came across as amusing and likeable (amazing!) It was then back to the mikes to thrash out *'Valerie'* which was a 'dup-tee-do, dup-tee-do' Kazoo triumph.

I'm not sure how the Prime Minister came across that day, but we all knew that we were the true headliners and once again he had to suffice in a supporting role. I don't know what became of David Cameron, I think he embarked on a downward spiral from that day forward, but not us, we were radio stars.

We had performed live on BBC Radio Solent to an estimated 272,000 listeners. OK this may be a tiny exaggeration, the weekly audience for Solent is estimated at 272,000 and I'm guilty of assuming that all of them were tuned in that afternoon.

Lovey hugs and showbiz air kisses all round and we left the studio for a glorious journey back along the M27 and a triumphal homecoming. A ticker tape welcome and open top bus tour round Gosport and along Lee-on-the-Solent seafront culminating in a free fry-up at the Penguin café was expected at the very least. Not really, but we did sing all the way home, we were buzzing. Our loved ones had heard us on the radio and loved it. Some had recorded the whole thing and this clip quickly went viral. Well it would have done had things gone viral back then. The only thing that had gone viral in our lifetimes was diphtheria and from my recollection that had received very few if any 'likes'. The by now famous clip was shared via the interwebnet thingy worldwide, well several cousins in Oz at least. On the back of this, the foodbank gig was a rip-roaring success, a total sell-out and we strummed along happily surrounded by a mountain of tins and packet food for the less fortunate people of Gosport.

There's no such thing as bad publicity is now our main motto.

I keep an archive of clippings about the Strummers and my favourite item is a print out from the show headlined "The Katie Martin show - featuring Prime Minister David Cameron and the Stokes Bay Strummers' a much-treasured memento of a great day out.

This isn't our only brush with fame or the famous. We've lorded it big time. It hasn't all been care homes where we've wangled a booking. For several years, we have blagged a slot at the biggest folk festival in these parts – the Wickham Festival. Wickham is a big deal for us since it attracts big names and big audiences. We have supported The Proclaimers, Steve Harley and Cockney Rebel, James Blunt, 10cc, Billy Bragg, Andy Fairweather-Low, The Stranglers, Chas and Dave. We also played at the final performance of the infamous Rolf Harris a few months prior to his trial and imprisonment – least said! Not bad for a small town uke group of restricted ambition and talent.

When I say 'supported' perhaps I should add that we've appeared on the same line up of the four-day festival. When I say 'line-up' perhaps I should add that the festival has four stages and we are always on stage four – the Community Stage. When I say 'stage' perhaps I should add that the Community Stage is in fact a tent strategically placed 20 metres into the festival site, just beyond the ticket desk and adjacent to the line-up of plastic port-a-loos.

Our first appearance at Wickham was at mid-day on day one – we were the very first act. We were promised that if we did well we would be promoted up the bill in subsequent years. We've now played the festival four times and we have achieved 1.30 pm on Day two – much better progress than the Solent Singers who remain stuck at mid-day Day One. Anyway, we don't mind performing early since it gets us a free 'performers wristband' to all the stages for the remainder of the day. No, the main disadvantage of been down the billing is that we are always below the waist in the nether regions of the Festival Souvenir T-shirts. All the group always buys a T-shirt with the headline act emblazoned across the chest area – 'THE

175

PROCLAIMERS' 'LEVEL 42' etc. Acts are then listed in ever decreasing font size down the T shirt. Just before the hem of the shirt you may discern in font size 2.5 'THE STOKES BAY STRUMMERS'. Fame for us wouldn't be headlining on stage one, we are not that ambitious and we wouldn't want to appear in the 10 pm dark in front of thousands of inebriated revellers – we'll leave that to our betters. Sufficient fame would stem from appearing above the waist line on the festival T-shirt – maybe next year.

We always choose our best songs for Wickham and everyone gets very serious and a bit uptight during our many practice sessions. We are always nervous because we invite friends and family along to swell the audience numbers. On our first performance, we were ready to play under the cover of the open fronted tent in front of largish crowd that had gathered outside during our sound check. We twanged our first chord of our signature tune 'Stokes Bay Strummers Strumming' and the heavens opened. It hadn't rained all summer but the monsoon wind and stair-rod rain was now whipping through the tent. The front row of Strummers, including our electric uke bass player, were getting soaked. I would love to report that the stoic audience stood their ground, donned festival pac-a-macs and stuck with us but no, even our friends and families made a run for cover and we did the whole set with no audience. I appreciate that music audiences can be fickle, but one would have thought and expected family to stand by us – no matter what. This was made more galling when the rain ended abruptly at the exact end of our set and it didn't rain again all festival weekend. Since that experience however, we have played to some good audiences at Wickham. People buy their entry tickets and we are on the first stage by the ticket office and they have no option but to walk over to us and we don't want them to walk past under any circumstances. Our task is to try and keep them stood in front of us and we generally achieve this and all who dwell have a good time.

The rest of the festival day is then spent soaking up the glory by staying in the blue and beige uniforms to bask in the glory of the gig whilst strutting around the site with sleeves rolled up to highlight their fluorescent performers' wristbands. The Strummers love a wrist-band. It separates them from the masses. It is a clear and highly visible label that they are a 'performer'. Strange, because for most of the

Strummers their only previous experience of a wrist-band is from a hospital before being taken down for prostate butchery, or whatever the female equivalent is. Even better than a wrist-band is a performers' necklace with a dog lead clip dangling on the end holding the magic 'performers pass'. Strummers love these and can be seen wearing them around the Supermarkets of Gosport for weeks after the event and even better they can be multi tasked to provide safe anchorage for bifocals to keep them close and at the ready – a real bonus.

It's amazing how we stand out from the average 'folkie' at the festival. You know the sort, straggly beards, bald head with a strangely incongruent pony tail sprouting out of the only square inch of scalp that can sustain any growth - and that's just the women – not really honest. It's as though they have opted for baldness on the proviso that one inch would be spared to push out the requisite pony tail. A bald pony with a greasy hairy tail would look ridiculous, so why would a human being choose to look like this is beyond us Strummers – we have gone bald gracefully – well the men anyway. Folk festival attendees always wear socks with sandals, that's the law. It's also the only place, apart from the continent of Asia and Gosport Primark, were one can get away with wearing brightly coloured patterned synthetic silk pantaloons and waistcoats. Folkies all proport to save the planet, hug trees, eat bean sprouts and nuts and drink soymilk. However, this can't be true. For a start the car park is full of gas belching diesel four by fours, the adjacent festival camping area is crammed with pre-emission testing old battered campervans and I can't see how this saves any of the planet. As for diet, look at the range of food outlets at any festival. Anything fried, from chips, grease burgers, leather sandals, socks and on one stall, pony tail hot dogs. No worries, we love than all really, and the Strummers have learned to avoid all this by wearing beige and blue and taking their own food in a nice packed lunch. Folkies also like real ale. This is a good thing and is officially approved by the Strummers who have been known to partake in a few scoops of Hampshire Grumble Belly ale as an aid to recovery and to ease the post gig trauma.

Apart from Wickham we've also supported Coldplay at the band stand in Fareham town centre. Fareham is the posher twin of Gosport. Again, we were supporting Coldplay, but typical of superstars they didn't show up. The reality was that Coldplay put their name to a mass national community musical band stand event and community groups simultaneously throughout the land played in local band stands. It was nice to play in Fareham to make them realise how much they are missing out by not living in Gosport. We also of course put a picture with caption on our website – '*Stokes Bay Strummers supporting Coldplay in Fareham*'

We also played at the Portsmouth Victorious Festival once. This is a massive festival and we managed to get on to the line-up because our tutor at the time oversaw one of the stages. We supported Charlotte Church (yes, we got a T-shirt) who headlined the main stage. A highlight for our nominated leader was queuing to register for the much-anticipated performers' necklaces and passes. Passes were hand-written and hand laminated, a time-consuming process for the impresario in charge, each taking about 5 minutes to complete. No real problem for the time rich solo artist that is Charlotte Church, but when our man reached the front of the queue however, the sighs were loud and deep when he announced he wanted twenty-seven passes. If only Charlotte had been behind, rather than in front of the Strummers. Still we eventually got the passes, one each for every Strummer to cherish and show to confused grand children in the future. We were ready to rock and roll and headed for the Real Ale Tent, not to booze, but to play to a wholly inebriated Sunday afternoon audience. The drink worked and we had a great time, probably one of our best gigs. The audience fuelled by real ale rocked, danced, and sang their heads off – a great buzz for all involved. We all stayed on to see Charlotte Church and can honestly say that we played to a louder and more appreciative audience than she did at that festival.

Talking of sharing a dressing room with Charlotte Church, we once shared a dressing room with a famous Scottish pipe band. So famous I've forgotten their name, or is there only one? We don't often get a dressing room. Truth is the beige and blue is best stored and donned in the privacy of one's own bedroom. Imagine our pre-gig excitement on being told we had a dressing room, even though we had to share. There's usually about twenty of us and our instruments are not very big or loud. It wasn't easy to count the actual number of pipers in the dressing room since the tartan was over whelming as a blurred vision of pixelated primary colours. I presume one could play bagpipes dressed in blue and beige, or is tartan the law? This visual invasion was however nothing compared to the audio maelstrom they produced on tuning up. I say 'tuning' advisably. How can anyone mock the lovely ukulele when bag pipes still exist. It had however the advantage of dulling our earing sufficiently so that we didn't hear our own set.

How many of you can remember which celebrity switched on the Christmas lights in your town last year? No luck, then I'll tell you, it was probably an extinguished soap star, a reality TV pseudo celeb or someone moonlighting from the cast of the local panto. Down here in Gosport we are not that fickle and yes, the Stokes Bay Strummers were chosen to play at the switching on of the Gosport Christmas lights one year. Well when I say Christmas lights I mean a Lidl rejected lop-sided fir tree inserted into the Town Hall patio at an angle of 60 degrees by council workmen. The tree starts out in November with about 50 feeble lights and by Christmas if we are lucky, 12 are still working. And because we are still in the EU (just), the home of all Health and Safety, the council always surround the 'tree' with two-meter crash barriers so no one can approach or actually see it, just in case the brilliance of the lights blinds a local drunk, or someone nicks the bulbs. Anyway, we played 'Mele Kalikimaka' which somehow lifted the whole event.

Fame doesn't come along easily, one must search it out. A keen Strummer and frustrated David Bowie groupie realised this and decided to organise our own Ukulele festival. No pony tails, no sandals with socks just beige and blue (or equivalent) and ukes. No tents and bad weather but inside the palatial local church. No unhealthy festival food, but good old afternoon tea and fancy cakes made by the WI. Years before our partners in uke crime and local friendly rivals 'The Pompey Pluckers' had organised a 'Pompulele' and despite everyone having to shout 'Pompulele' every 30 seconds it had been very successful. We are Gosport and we knew we could do better, so one brave Strummer organised GUMF – The Gosport Ukulele Music Festival. Gosport for one summers day became the centre of uke world. More than ten uke groups played and the day ended in a mass strum in and sing along. Gosport and the

Strummers shared 30 seconds of fame courtesy of local BBC TV – a great success.

Chapter Thirteen – Democracy in the SBS

The strap line on the Stokes Bay Strummers web page reads 'We are a ukulele group who play for fun'. Most of the time the group is fun; on occasions, it's akin to root canal work without the anaesthesia. I have spent as many hours unable to sleep worrying about 'that bloody ukulele group' (wife's words') as I ever did in my professional working life – and believe me I had a very challenging and stressful job.

"Why oh why should this be?

The group is fun.

This is retirement, this is leisure.

I'm doing it because I want to do it.

No one is forcing me.

Pack it in. I can't, I love it.

I love the group, I love the uke, I love the Strummers.

Why are some people so bloody difficult?

Why doesn't everyone just do as I say?

Why isn't everyone like me?

I'm a 'founder member' so it's my right to be right."

Differences arise in two broad areas, firstly, musical differences, usually around song choice, and secondly, organisational tensions. The group has up to thirty members. Trying to get thirty people to pull together musically and organisationally can get a little fraught at times. How should an organisation of about thirty people be run? The Strummers group is about the same size as a small to medium business. Members commit many hours to it. Money is involved, members pay 'subs', tutors and room hire has to be paid for and thousands of pounds is collected for local charities. In short it could become a very serious business and this isn't fun. Alternatively, it could simply be left to run itself. Over the years both extremes have been tried, and many other versions between, and the group runs on regardless. The group can go for months in perfect harmony (sorry, not musically, but at least not tearing each other's throats out) then something crops up and we get tears, more tears and then a demoralising flurry of e-mail assassinations.

Is democracy over rated or is it the answer. Not the binary Brexit or Prime Minister's question time style of democracy but a softer more caring more participative democracy. A bit like the old Lib Dems before they sold their soul for power. A democracy where everyone is equal, including the founder members, whatever their uke colour, plectrum type, strumming style, singing voice or punctuality and yes, even those who still for some strange reason bring along banjo ukes.

When I was in full time employment, the office door of the organisation next to my company had a large sign that said '.... where people flourish'. I always wanted to walk in through that door. I wanted to flourish. This wasn't helped when some jester put a sign on our door that said ...where people perish! 'The Stokes Bay Strummers ... where people flourish' that's what we need.

Some Strummers still long for those innocent early days. I wonder if Steve Jobs or Mark Zuckerberg wish they were still in an organisation that could fit into a small garden shed, when six people could run everything including making lunches and organising the tea boat. Maybe that's the issue the Stokes Bay Strummers have reached a Microsoft or Facebook corporate level. If this is the case, then I'm all for floating the whole thing. Not on the stock market but on the Solent. Small was beautiful and in the early days, the founder members of The Strummers achieved perfect harmony. It was easy since all six or seven members had a say and we moved forward in unison. This all began to change as the group grew.

To cope with the growing numbers, it was decided to have a committee. Yes, a committee, that truly dreadful word. I agree with the wag who said 'the optimum committee is one that has no members. I bet that Steve and Mark don't run their organisations by committee. The first Stokes Bay Strummers committee members were the founder members and not surprisingly this was the time that the term 'founder member' became so hated within the group. The Committee made decisions, the group probably agreed with the decisions but would never admit to it. The group didn't accept the decisions because they hadn't been involved and very quickly a 'us' and 'them' schism set in. Someone once said that 'the human race divides into those who people who want to be controlled and those who have no such desire'. Strummers want to be controlled, but in a way that makes them think they are not. One bright spark had the idea of calling the committee a 'working group' in the vain hope that this would heal the schism. Working group was what it was. It was a group of people who did all the work. The remainder of the group simply turned up to strum or to moan in the belief that it all happened organically, that no one had to do any work, just turn up strum and sing – happiness sorted.

We will never be the size of Microsoft but we still have 'work' to be done, it doesn't run itself. Remember this is fun, this is voluntary, this is retirement and this is a large part of many older people's social lives. It can't be prescriptive or authoritarian it must be gentle and covertly coercive to run the group in a seamless non-controversial manner to keep everyone smiling and happy.

Some Strummers are retired from senior management positions. They've been planners and they like, and need a plan, but with the Strummers it must be a simple plan for it to succeed. Basically, it's about getting enough Strummers booted and suited to the right gig, on the right day, in the right venue, with the right equipment and music and at the right time.

A good start for all our activity is the gig book. A paper A4 diary passed round at each practice session. It's not rocket science, put your name in the book if you can make the gig. Written in the book are the details of what to wear (remember we are fixated on wearing beige and blue uniforms) the date, time, duration, and venue address – and the Post Code for those Strummers brave enough to use a Sat Nav. Apparently even this is too complex for some. Strummers put their names in the book, then either forget or choose to ignore it. Some have commitment issues and don't decide until the gig day. Maybe they're waiting to see if the 'Pointless' jackpot goes or who wins 'Cash in the Attic' and these members turn up if and when they feel like it. Some are too self-important to put their names in the book and believe that it's obvious that they need to be there since how could the Strummers perform without them. The result being that no one knows how many Strummers are likely to turn up for each gig and the lady who runs the book lives on the edge of despair. Of course, there's the website with this information but accessing it on a regular basis is too far into the dark side for some Strummers. Luckily, we've never been seriously embarrassed due to lack of numbers but it's been close on occasions. We've had Strummers turn up having forgotten their ukuleles and we always get someone in blue and beige when we are supposed to be in dark trousers shirts and waistcoats and vice versa.

Keeping the song sheets up to date is probably the most thankless Strummers task. Some poor bugger has the job of trying to keep tabs on the many changes inflicted on the songs in practice and producing a definitive agreed version. Do you remember the Herman's Hermits classic *'I'm into Something Good'*? We love this song, but we have been trying to pin down an ending for it for four years. Each practice session appears to result in a different ending to the song. Should it be 'Something Good – Oh yeah Something good' repeated three times or four? It's been three on many occasions, it's been four and then back to three. It oscillates between the two. Frustrated song keeper tells everyone to make a pencil note of the changes as they emerge. The result is that each Strummers music sheet looks like a getaway plan for a failed bank robbery written by a dyslexic whose first language is not English. Most Strummers are so confused that two-thirds of the way into the song they simply give up playing and singing and leave the ending to those who know better – which is usually no one - and even song keeper man has lost the will to live on this one. If every strummer had printed out every new and 'final' version of *I'm into Something Good'* the worlds' paper forests would be totally depleted. I dread to think what that nice Peter Noone aka Herman (or his Hermits) would think, but I wish he would pitch up one Tuesday evening and let us know how the bloody song should end. You may be thinking why not just listen and watch the song on YouTube?   Good idea, but remember we are not the Hermits, we are the Stokes Bay Strummers and we must have our own special version.   Anyway, Peter Noone was in Coronation Street (not many people know that by the way) so probably doesn't even know himself how the bloody song ends.

Choosing the songs for the set list for each gig is also a controversial task and in the past, we have shared this to give more people the chance to have their favourites on the list. Liberal democracy in action!

A further remaining controversial issue is the content and style of the Tuesday practice session. All the group agree that we have two sessions per week. Most agree that Tuesdays is about improvement and getting gig ready and Thursdays is about fun and having a good old unrestrained strum and sing along. This is how it is. Problems arise when those who only attend 'fun' turn up at gigs without the knowledge and practice covered on improvement night and of course some want 'fun' on both nights – and why not.

On Tuesdays, we have a paid tutor. For this we each pay two pounds for his time. Our current tutor is talented, qualified, enthusiastic, and amazingly - young. The Stokes Bay Strummers have undoubtedly improved musically through his wise counsel. For two pounds, we get a graduate musician and trained teacher. Two pounds is too much for some, and a minority refuse to attend and some amazingly have even walked away from the group over this issue. Our current tutor also works in a local recording studio and my only criticism of him is that he's never volunteered to produce and record a new CD with us. This is understandable however since he's heard all about the first effort and is therefore probably wise to maintain and protect his reputation in the industry.

We've had other tutors in the past, not least the infamous music shop owner in Gosport. We also had a professional sea shanty singer who took to conducting us from a lectern with a proper conducting stick thing – a total waste, since as already discussed no Strummer ever looks up. Our conductor could have been fending off pirates with a sword or painting a modern art masterpiece and we wouldn't have known. So, a bit of a waste really and he left to grow his hair and beard to tour the world on tall sailing ships, paying his way by singing sea shanties.

We've had a uke rocker pony tail balding head tutor for a short while but he spent the whole time trying to teach us very impressive complex intro licks to all our songs and thus blew the brains and finger tips of most Strummers within hours. A very nice man

194

and no one knows what happened to him. He was an excellent uke player so maybe it's him that plays the catchy uke riffs on all those TV ads now - I hope it is him, he'd be good at that.

We also advertised for a tutor at one time. Only one candidate applied and we invited him along to observe a Tuesday session to see what he thought and how he could help. He came along and we gave him our song book and he sat to one side and listened intently as we played. We were all on our best behaviour and to be honest a little bit nervous. It must have been very much like the time that George Martin went along to have a look at the Beatles or when Malcolm McLaren was considering taking on the Pistols. I'm sure that Sid Vicious and Mr Rotten would have had a few nerves, and we did too. At the end of the session the candidate said he was impressed and yes, he could help us. The Strummers however didn't take this at face value and they wanted to know what qualifications our candidate had. After all we were musicians by now and we couldn't possibly have an unqualified person teaching us anything. 'Oh yes' replied the candidate, 'I have a PSV licence'. I think most of us knew what a PSV was, but some looked puzzled as they tried to resolve these initials into something related to music.   Our one and only candidate to become our tutor thought apparently, that what we needed was a bus driver – Passenger Service Vehicle! As it happens we had an excellent bus driver already so our song book keeper swiped back our song book and showed our crest fallen candidate the door. Local rumours persist that he's since applied for the England football managers job since they obviously need a bus driver to get them to matches. Apparently, he got that job and now has a better win ratio than Roy Hodgson.

Our recruitment had failed and has never been attempted since. To fill the gap someone suggested that we take turns to be tutor. We don't need to pay, we can do it ourselves. This worked OK for a while and we had some fun but Strummers were generally too shy to step forward. One person volunteered and did a good job for a time before the Strummers stopped listening and started misbehaving and the sessions began to disintegrate and our volunteer wisely threw the towel in. It's still the case however that some in the group would go back to this rather than pay two measly pounds for a professional tutor. We still have a minority that prefer to bash their way through a song and move on, even if the singing and playing is all over the place. Some don't appreciate trying to improve, trying to get each song the best it can be and most of all playing as a group, rather than as a bunch of individuals.

Democracy is stretched and problems occur whenever money is involved. Jeremy Corbyn would have been proud had he attended one of our many talk shop meetings/committees. One member suggested that those with more money should pay more subs. Please note that we are only talking about subs of three or four pounds per week, two pounds for the tutor, the remainder for the hire of the Guide Hut. But our George Osborne look alike had learned that some Strummers were in receipt of an additional pension on top of their state pension and asked, and he was serious, that subscription levels should be means tested and tiered depending on ability to pay. This was quashed quickly when one person, with two pensions, angrily volunteered to pay everyone's subs, every week, and this generous offer shamed austerity George into submission – although he subsequently left the group – the moaning strummer not George

Osborne, he was never in the Strummers, that was David Cameron!

It doesn't seem to matter how much we pay each week the cash builds and we always have a surplus (unlike Mr Osborne – ha!). We achieve this surplus due to the loyal wife of one of our Strummers. Loyal strummer's wife attends every practice session and every gig to support her loved one – a picture of married bliss and dedication. She's heard more ukulele than is good for anyone but her loyalty is unabashed. This had to be rewarded, we couldn't just let her sit there on the side for hour after hour whilst her hubby had all the fun. A role had to be found for her within the democracy that is the Stokes Bay Strummers. She'd accepted and done well in the key role of blowing the train whistle in Chattanooga Choo Choo, albeit still sat on the side and refusing to sit within the group. This wasn't enough, she's got talent and that talent should be harvested for the good of the group - but doing what? Then one week our treasurer was away on another cruise and we needed someone to take the subs. Since becoming treasurer he'd coincidently taken to cruising and expensive foreign holidays about six times a year. I worked as an auditor for a while and 'the treasurer is away on another cruise' is not a phrase that sits well. We believe that this was because he'd retired from work, and not because he had access to the Strummers bank book – we hoped anyway. Anyway, loyal wife took this role and since that day everyone pays their subs, they have no choice, no one dare not pay and the book she keeps would not be out of place in the Government Audit Office. We now have better control of our finances than any government agency. Next time we see David Cameron we should tell him that we've found the next Chancellor of the Exchequer. Although in reality we may never see Dave again. Since he was kicked out of office, after the Brexit debacle, he hasn't appeared with any uke groups. Maybe he's strumming in his shed or lonely bedroom biding his time till there's a suitable vacancy for his talents.

Due to good subs collection, we usually have a surplus of cash and how to spend this always tests our democratic commitment. Some rightly argue that we could reduce the subs to two pounds a week. A sound idea but even if it was free and came with triple Nectar points the paying the tutor moaners would still stay away. After democratic votes, we've spent surplus cash on a next to useless PA system and we've also part funded Strummers social events such as a skittle evening with chicken in the basket. Yes, in Gosport they still serve chicken in a basket in the belief that this is haute cuisine. Social events like this can be a bit fraught because Strummers are parted from their loved ones, not their spouses or partners, but their ukes. A Strummers' evening without ukes and strumming is beyond the comprehension and durability of most members. The long-suffering Strummers' spouses are not usually keen to attend social evenings since they've become accustomed to the thrill of having the TV remote to themselves on practice nights to catch up on Holby City in the peace and quiet gained by kicking a uke player out for the evening. The future of the surplus then is unsure at the time of writing. It's not yet sufficient to balance the country's deficit but unless we can agree what to spend it on soon it may get to that.

We did receive a small cash grant from our County Council one year in recognition of our sterling contribution to the local community. This was eventually spent on shiny blue imitation silk waistcoats imported from Asia through eBay. This decision caused consternation among the Strummers. Some didn't think it right that we accept public tax payers' money, others thought, if we don't have it than the cash will only go to some other group so why not us. Some even moaned that the constant friction of their strumming arm would too easily erode the cheap tacky imitation silk frontage on the waistcoats. During this exercise in democracy the council needed a receipt to prove what we had spent the cash on. The prevarication made this difficult and the 'working group' came very close to telling the council to stick their money.

In 2013, the Strummers were nominated by the Portsmouth News for a 'We can do it' community award which was nice. About twenty Strummers turned up at the King's Theatre Portsmouth for the award ceremony with acceptance speeches crafted and ready, only to be beaten by a local dog walking group. Outrageous and made a hundred times worse by the fact that our arch rivals The Pompey Pluckers, although not nominated for an award themselves, had been invited to play and did a great set to entertain the crowd.

We play for charity and this money is kept separate. Every penny we earn goes to our chosen annual charity and selecting a charity is always democratic. The Strummers prefer local charities with low overheads and over the past four or so years the Strummers have earned more than sixteen grand and donated this to some fantastic local causes. All Strummers are exceptionally proud of this and rightly so. On reflection, this has probably become the raison-d'etre for the group and drives all members. We could probably forget the ukes and the music now and stand on street corners shaking collection tins.

Cash must be collected and accounted for, songs must be chosen and song sheets produced and maintained, gigs booked and set lists produced, Strummers must be herded to gigs, practice venues, tutors and sessions organised; and as in most community volunteer groups a handful of people do this work whilst the rest jog along happily or moan. The 'Working Group' worked for a while before imploding in the face of one or two moaners but democracy called and it was decided to hold an annual meeting to set our direction. This annual meeting is a psychologist dream and must be observed to be believed.

Strummers always turn up for the annual meeting. Even those long forgotten, even the disenchanted, even the ones who refuse to pay their subs, they all turn up to have their say. A couple of our better organised Strummers circulate a draft agenda for people to add to or comment on, and no one does. The meeting sets out with the aim of following the agreed agenda – all very PC and committee like. The Strummers sit in a circle, all very inclusive, and one of our MCs takes the chair and begins. The meeting is scheduled to last 45 minutes so Strummers bring their ukes because the Guide Hut is booked for an hour and a half so there will be time for some uking after the meeting. A big mistake since as already mentioned a Strummer with a uke on his lap or anywhere near his fingers cannot resist strumming it. To counter this one year, the Chair armed herself with an enormous old fashioned honk-honk car horn and a millisecond before a stray strum appeared she 'HONK HONKED' in the lug hole of the offender – not very PC nor inclusive but very effective. In subsequent years Strummers left their ukes at home to avoid temptation and the hearing damage. However, the horn was taken a step further and became used for anyone speaking in what the Chair considered out of turn. Not very PC nor inclusive and its use may just have stifled free speech and debate a little bit. In fact, Clement Atlee, who may or may not have been a uke player but was a Prime Minister, once said "Democracy means government by discussion, but it is only effective if you can stop people talking" perhaps he needed a horn. Although thinking about it imagine Prime Ministers' questions if the speaker had a honk-honk horn – much more interesting I think.

Thirty seconds into the meeting, and after three honks to obliterate stray strumming and four honks to drown out inappropriate verbal inputs, the agenda went out of the window and the meeting disintegrated into the usual annual two hours' discussion about subs, song choice, plectrum use, PA systems and charity choice. Members of the Stokes Bay Strummers love talking almost as much as the love uking, and many times more than they love listening. Amazingly however decision are made, minutes distributed and the Strummers strum on happily for a few months after each annual meeting.

The Stokes Bay Strummers are a lovely bunch of lovely people and it is this 'soft' version of democracy that keeps them ticking along very nicely. The group has its characters and differences but these are usually celebrated rather than bemoaned. The group has married couples whose domestic life must be doubly uke obsessed. The average age of the Strummers must be over well over 60 and several are over 80. Some hard-core Strummers have been with the group since its conception or very shortly after. New members join, some stay and others leave after witnessing a few weeks of our practice sessions. Younger people tend not to stick with us, which is a shame, but understandable considering our choice of gigs, songs, and our average age. Younger people also have busy lives which is not the case for all Strummers. The group has undoubtedly provided a great pastime, much fun, and a big social service to many members.

Strummers have left because they've moved home or become ill and we've had one very sad passing of a key and much loved strummer. A few have left because they've had enough of gigging and the commitment is too much. A small number have left due to musical or organisational differences and one has formed another uke group in Gosport which is grand. The vast majority of ex Strummers left on good terms and still keep in touch which is good. There's only been one instance where a person has been asked to leave and this caused much upset among the group which is sad and some would like the person concerned to return, which is unlikely. These things happen in any organisation and its part of life unfortunately.

I think that the lives and times of the Stokes Bay Strummers would make a great TV reality show or sitcom. 'Made in Gosport' or 'The Only Way Is Uke' live on TV five times a week. Each episode following the trials and tribulations of the Stokes Bay Strummers and its characters. A full episode could feature one of our oldest Strummers, a great character who's bald but with hair two feet long, wears denim dungarees, drives a thirty-year-old Rover car, and has England's only outdoor full size open air snooker table. One of our married couples could fill an episode portraying married uke bliss. Then there's all the sad cases of Ukulele Acquisition Syndrome which could bring added drama through the sad tears of long suffering and financially challenged Strummers spouses. Perhaps this illness of owning too many ukes could be featured on a '24 hours in A and E' special or 'Trust me I'm a Uke Doctor'.

Of course, we do have characters and characteristics that wouldn't warrant this publicity. There's always one or more in any group of people and we have suffered from negativity at times. There's a Native American proverb that says 'Never criticise a man until you've walked a mile in his moccasins'. This is apt for Strummers at times since a minority do tend to over criticise and under contribute – but this is rare thankfully. It is very dis-heartening to spend much effort over many hours to produce for example a new song only to have it shot down and totally dismissed by one of the resident Victor Meldrews. Much better to try it and work together to improve it. I do remember one individual who's first words, as he was getting out of his car, before he'd even entered the room, would be something like 'you know that new song – chords are all wrong, it's rubbish'. We've also had people not turn up because they don't like a song that we are practicing or playing. A few years ago, one of our favourite songs was '16 Tons', you know the one, *'16 tons and what do you get, another day older and deeper in debt'*. Unfortunately, when our then tutor taught us the riff for this song he got it wrong, but most of us liked it. This got worse since we transposed the incorrect riff melody to the whole song. Great, we had our own version of '16 Tons' and 99 per cent of the group loved it. One Strummer however didn't. '16 Tons' was his favourite song and he spent weeks playing the real version to us and singing the real tune despite what the remainder of the group were singing. The group turned this man's favourite song into a nightmare for him. If '16 Tons' was on the play list, he wasn't interested and would not turn up. When he moved away from the area we marked the occasion and said farewell by writing our own version and singing a very special song for him. Yes, you guessed, a wrong tune version of '16 Tons'.

He's got sixteen ukes, the star of our set

Another Strummer off to deepest Dorset

Big Michael, don't you leave us, please don't go

*...cos you collect the subs and yer sing real
low*

More than six feet high, his train whistle wet

Another tune ruined - the worst in the set

Big Michael when you leave, can I please blow

...yer old train whistle, in a Ukulele show

He's got sixteen tons of furniture to shift

Another box packed, too heavy to lift

*Big Michael, don't you leave us, please don't
go*

*...cos you'll miss the Strummers in yer new
bung-a–low*

We sing Sixteen tons, and what do we get

Another song ruined - and we're deep in regret

Big Michael, don't you leave us, no need to go

*.. we'll fix this tune for our next uke show etc
etc....*

I can honestly say that I don't like most the songs we play. I would not choose to add any of our songs to my Spotify play list, but they are mostly good group uke songs and give our audiences much pleasure - so accept them for what they are. Its democracy!

Chapter Fourteen – Ukulele Oblivion

The future of the ukulele is secure. People are living longer and healthier later lives. Add to this the tiny and relatively inexpensive instrument that makes people smile whenever they see, hear, or play it, and it's fun and laughter all the way. We are living in Ukulele boom time and the uke is cool.

There are many different things that can happen that create a cause for laughter. Laughing at yourself is perhaps one of the best character traits a person can have. Being part of a group like the Stokes Bay Strummers is most of the time about fun and laughter. It will remain so providing the urge to take itself too seriously is supressed whenever it arises. Retirement needs to be about trying new things. Whether its parasailing in the Caribbean or taking a campervan to John O' Groats you're certain to have fun somewhere along the way. With retirement comes more time to join clubs and groups. Anytime you put yourself in the company of other people, fun things happen at some point. Doctors should in my opinion be writing fewer prescriptions for pills, and more for joining a uke group. Laughter is the best medicine and being in a ukulele group provides lots of laughter.

The most misunderstood thing about the ukulele is that it's supposed to sound a bit rubbish. It's only got four strings and these are tuned in a strange way so it's bound to sound a little bit odd. Young people are now playing ukuleles, although not in the Stokes Bay Strummers unfortunately. Uke is cool. A new generation is playing uke, and this generation don't associate it with the old times. They don't know who George Formby is, instead they've grown up hearing ukuleles in punk bands, in reggae and in the sound track to many films and TV shows. In recent times, there's been a shortage of ukuleles to buy. Most now come from China or the Far East and even these masters of mass cheap production have been unable to satisfy the insatiable demand word-wide for ukes. Don't wait for China, no need to hop on a cruise to Hawaii why not make your own or buy second hand. Don't spend too much, but get a Uke – everyone should have at least one in the home – or shed – especially if you've retired!

In the UK, there are now uke festivals all summer long. One respected uke site lists more than 300 uke clubs across the country from 'The Ukes of Allonby' through to 'Wukulele Worthing'. There's probably many times more than this and there will be a uke club within travelling distance of where you live and it will be a fun group to join – guaranteed. Uke clubs are taking over the world. There's a uke groups in many countries from Canada, Malaysia, New Zealand, Australia, Europe and beyond. Who knows one day there could be Strummers in Aleppo, Mosul or Kabul. If I'm expelled from the Stokes Bay Strummers (after the group read this book) then I would join the Ukuhooley Dublin. I would pick this one from the name and location alone. I don't know, but in my imagination, this must be a top fun Guinness fuelled, pub based warm Irish sing along group.

You may be familiar with Shakespeare's 'The Seven Ages of Man'? (if so, well done, not only a ukulele lover but well-read also).

The Seven Ages are very apt to the development of the Stokes Bay Strummers. We've had a successful conception and birth where we had a great time setting up the group. Perhaps this was the most enjoyable stage, not surprising since being at the conception and birth of anything is an amazing time. Our founder members are guilty of rose coloured glasses in this aspect but the genie is now out of the bottle and the Stokes Bay Strummers can't be born-again, can they?

The group stuttered through infancy when, as Shakespeare would say, 'we were helpless babies who knew little'. The innocence of this time was pure joy akin to a toddler learning to walk and talk at the same time.

We've survived the 'whining schoolboy phase' as we went to uke lessons and reverted to misbehaving school children.

We were 'lovers and soldiers' and became easily aroused and hot headed as we tried to make a reputation for ourselves even at the cost of foolish risks. More than 250 gigs are testament to the love and soldiering spirit of the group.

We're acquiring wisdom along the journey and have gained prosperity and social status. We may also have become a little vain as we've begun to enjoy the finer things of life such as too many expensive ukes.

The average age of the Stokes Bay Strummers is well over 60 and most members of the group are now approaching or are in, old age. Shakespeare warns that at this stage in life one can become a shell of one's former self, physically and mentally and begin to become the butt of others' jokes, lose firmness and assertiveness, and shrink in stature and personality. Incapacity may then closely follow when one becomes dependent on others for care and are unable to interact with the world, the final destination being mere oblivion.

Our Strummers strum on well into their eighties and it's a fantastic thing to witness their contribution. Eighty-year-old Strummers entertaining audiences of other eighty year olds – brilliant. I don't think the Stokes Bay Strummers are destined for 'oblivion' Mister Shakespeare, but the group needs

215

younger people to keep it going. Perhaps the Government could reduce the retirement age so that more people have more time to do things such as community ukulele groups instead of getting people to work till they drop.

Writing this whimsical, tongue in cheek story of the Stokes Bay Strummers has been pure joy and brought back so many good memories. I also had the privilege to share and learn more about some of stories from one of our founder members, Alan, who sadly passed away last year. It was sharing this time with Alan as he was terminally ill that inspired me to write this book. I had no choice, he told me he would haunt me if I didn't – thanks Alan.

Printed in Great Britain
by Amazon